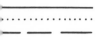

F WEBB CHILES

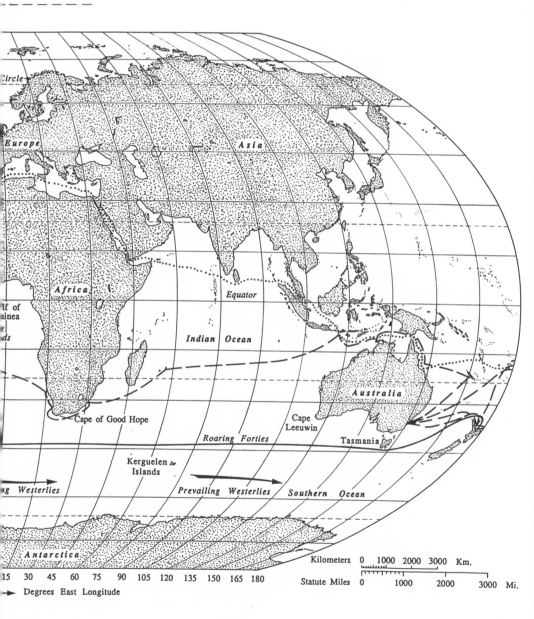

Also by Webb Chiles

Storm Passage

The Open Boat

The Ocean Waits

A SINGLE WAVE

STORIES OF STORMS AND SURVIVAL

Webb Chiles

S

SHERIDAN HOUSE

First published 1999 by
Sheridan House Inc.
145 Palisade Street
Dobbs Ferry, NY 10522

Library of Congress Cataloging-in-Publication Data

Chiles, Webb.
    A single wave : stories of storms and survival / Webb Chiles.
        p.   cm.
    ISBN 1-57409-072-0 (alk. paper)
    1. Chiles, Webb.   2. Voyages around the world.   I. Title.
  G420.C475A3   1999
  910.4'5'092—dc21   99-10828
                                                                CIP

Edited by Janine Simon
Designed by Jesse Sanchez

Printed in the United States of America

ISBN   1-57409-072-0

To Carol,
the love I hoped for
and to
Bill and Hemmie Gilmore,
whose kindness was in normal terms extraordinary
but for them was only normal

A ship in port is safe, but that's not what ships are built for.
  —**Grace Murray Hopper**

My soul, your voyages have been your native land.
  —**Nikos Kazantzakis**

Curtis probably never found out either [why Two Whistles, a Crow chief, had a crow on his head when Curtis photographed him], because after thirty-three years in the field taking photos of the Indians he went crazy and was placed in an asylum. When they let him go he went down to Old Mexico and looked for gold, with a diffidence in recovery that characterized the behavior of many great men—let's go to the edge and jump off again.
  —**Jim Harrison, DAHLVA**

(I) am, I believe, following the clear path of my fate. Always to be pushing out like this, beyond what I know cannot be the limits— what else should a man's life be? Especially an old man who has, by a clear stroke of fortune, been violently freed of the comfortable securities that make old men happy to sink into blindness, deafness, the paralysis of all desire, feeling, will. What else should our lives be but a continual series of beginnings, of painful settings out into the unknown, pushing off from the edges of consciousness into the mystery of what we have not yet become, except in dreams that blow in from out there bearing the fragrance of islands we have not sighted.
  —**David Malouf, AN IMAGINARY LIFE**

A sailor is an artist whose medium is the wind.
  —**Webb Chiles**

CONTENTS

I was just rereading my correspondence with Webb Chiles, which dates back to 1976. The hundreds of letters between us record life lived at a level of intensity most people couldn't sustain. More than anyone I've ever met, Webb seeks to establish his limits. This life direction has nothing to do with morality or judgment. It has to do with a wish to measure endurance. Webb wants to know what his mind and body can take—how much, for how long.

Webb's first piece, published in the July 1977 issue of *SAIL*, sets the proper tone for his subsequent 22 years: "Saturday morning, November 2, 1974. I left San Diego, California, to sail around the world without an engine and alone as quickly as possible. I was born for this moment and for all the days ahead . . . I am about to undergo an ordeal. But I have . . . no illusions. I expect an ordeal, an ordeal of grandeur."

In this book the reader begins to understand an extraordinary character, what we say about special boats in the sailing business, a 'one-of-kind'. What especially sets Webb apart from other extraordinary characters is his ability to write about what is happening within and without himself with objective clarity, as if he were watching someone else.

Take his first ordeal, for example. He tried three times before he made it around Cape Horn for the first time. He finally rounded it to set a then world record for the fastest solo circumnavigation in a monohull. As he says in a letter to me dated May 11, 1982: "The ocean has always been for me a testing place for the spirit." And that was the grandeur in the ordeal—getting high marks on the test, by his own system of scoring.

Reading the EGREGIOUS chapters in this book the reader first sees Webb's ability to watch himself at work. On his third try for the Cape Horn his hull cracked in a gale near the Equator. So he bailed his way east through cyclones, through capsizes, through cold and wet terror. Never does he quite lose his sense of humor; as he remarks at one point, ". . . for a hot shower and an uninterrupted night's sleep, I would gladly sell my somewhat tarnished soul. The Devil is never around when you really want him."

Webb tested his spirit again by setting off in 1978 to circumnavigate the world in an 18-foot, 9-inch undecked yawl. He named this British-built stock Drascombe Lugger CHIDIOCK TICHBORNE, after the man who wrote a poem Webb admired. Not incidentally, Tichborne wrote the poem the night he was executed. The only problem, Webb notes in the small-yawl chapter, was "fitting a nineteen-foot name on an eighteen-foot boat."

Webb set another record—for being the first person to cross the Pacific in an open boat. His voyage across the Indian Ocean (4,058 miles from Singapore to Aden in 47 days) was at the time the longest nonstop passage in an open boat. People like Webb—and there aren't very many—always astonish me. Sometimes on purpose, sometimes almost in spite of himself, Webb Chiles rubs against the edges of risk. With his eyes open he pushes at life, and at death.

When he took off in the open boat, we at *SAIL* worried about the 'stunt' factor. Should we publish stories by this man? Was this sailing or was it circus performing? He carried no flares, no safety gear, no EPIRB in the little yawl. "I don't want people looking for me if I sink," he said. This was a man on his own, in every sense.

Although he loved CHIDIOCK TICHBORNE and thought her an excellent seaworthy craft, Webb came even closer to dying in the little yawl than he had in EGREGIOUS. On the way to Papua New Guinea from Fiji, CHIDIOCK is pitchpoled and swamped 300 miles west of Fiji and Webb is adrift for two weeks. Finally he reaches Vanuatu and is swept over the reef—this is sheer luck—to land on a beach, more or less intact. Indefatigable as ever, he repairs the boat and sails on.

Then, when beating up the Red Sea, he goes aground on a reef in Saudi Arabia, is arrested, and jailed as a spy. He is finally released, but the Saudis keep the boat. He gets another Drascombe Lugger in England, ships it to Egypt, and then sails down the Red Sea to pick up CHIDIOCK 's track. Webb completed his second circumnavigation aboard CHIDIOCK II for the most part, but not entirely. The boat was driven ashore in the Canary Islands and, with typical Chiles unpredictability, he decided to leave her there.

In the meantime, overlapping with the CHIDIOCK saga, in 1983 he bought RESURGAM, a 36-foot Sparkman & Stephens-designed sloop, and completed his third circumnavigation in her, closing the circle in the Marquesas Islands.

He continued sailing in RESURGAM west to Australia, and then east, returning to Cape Horn, the scene of his terrible trials in EGREGIOUS. Then he sailed to Uruguay, Rio de Janeiro, on up the Caribbean and to Florida. Once you've returned to the spot—Cape Horn—where for the first time you were able to stop for a moment, emotionally stilled, what do you do next? Where do you go?

What Webb did was observe his boat sinking. In August 1992, about 10 miles off Fort Lauderdale, he "pulled the plug at midnight," watched RESURGAM go down, and then he began swimming. Eventually he found himself swimming for his life, in both senses—emotional and physical. He was in the water about 26 hours without a life jacket before he was rescued by fishermen. As he says, the "animal in myself" kept him alive. These were the depths that were left to him.

This chapter, 'Swimming', is perhaps the most moving in the book. Even at the edge of sanity, Webb watches himself watching his beloved boat—this was the boat he loved over all others—sinking, murdered by his own hand. Even here, his black humor is alive: "The engine was almost brand-new . . . I had thought when we repowered in Australia that this engine should last the rest of my life, and so it would."

Webb is very strong, and the epilogue of his book concerns itself with his returning to life. With his last money he buys HAWKE and in 1993 sails from New York to Key West, crossing RESURGAM's track.

Now Webb lives in Boston, aboard the renamed HAWKE OF TUONELA, where he is outfitting her so he can resume his fourth circumnavigation. This is the plan. And so far, in all but one instance, Webb has done what he has planned.

Patience Wales
SAIL Magazine, 1998

Tolstoy begins *Anna Karenina* by declaring that every happy family is alike, but every unhappy family is unhappy in its own way.

I don't know if there are more happy than unhappy families. Perhaps there are. But at sea there are certainly many more pleasant, uneventful days than there are storms. Even at Cape Horn, in the stormiest season, gales are likely only one day out of three. A peculiarity of human nature is that no one much cares to read about happy families or fine sailing.

Not long ago I happened across a sentence in an article by Rod Kulbach. In passing Mr. Kulbach wrote: "I am awed by Webb Chiles 'tales of survival'." This caused me to realize that no matter how I view my life, I am best known for those 'tales of survival'.

So here are the dramatic highlights of a quarter century in three boats: EGREGIOUS, a 37-foot cutter; CHIDIOCK TICHBORNE, an 18-foot open undecked yawl; and RESURGAM, a 36-foot sloop. In these boats I made more than three circumnavigations, twice alone, twice setting world records, twice via Cape Horn, which I was the first American to round alone.

The stories include capsizes in a cyclone in the Tasman and in a storm in the Southern Ocean; Force 12 winds off Cape Horn; drifting for two weeks and three hundred miles in the South Pacific after a swamping west of Fiji; a twenty-six-hour swim in the Gulf Stream covering about one hundred and thirty miles after a sinking off Florida; and enough other troubles in exotic climes from Tahiti to the Red Sea to South Africa to Bali to New Jersey to cause one to take a serious interest in gardening.

You will not find any sea monsters here, or even monstrous waves. Most people, certainly most sailors, exaggerate, perhaps forgivably because of heightened emotions and limited experience, perhaps less forgivably because of inherent mendacity. I take pride in not exaggerating. Whenever possible I have sought out objective reports, as I did of Cyclone Colin in the meteorological office in Auckland, New Zealand.

As those few who have sailed with me know, if anything I underestimate. I do not dispute that fifty or sixty foot waves can exist. I just don't claim to have seen one. The biggest waves in these pages are estimated at twenty to thirty feet. They may have been more. But that is big enough.

What you will find here is life which can change very quickly into a struggle for survival, sometimes without warning, sometimes in the passing of a single wave.

As I write this I am fifty-six years old. I come from lines of mostly only children. It is very odd that I am the first man in my family in several generations to have reached even age forty, for I am the one who took the greatest risks.

Not later than three years from now, before my sixtieth birthday, I will resume my fourth circumnavigation, long interrupted by the sinking of RESURGAM. I will sail south to Africa and east to Australia, where I will complete this circle when I reach Sydney, Australia. Gardening pales.

Aboard THE HAWKE OF TUONELA
Boston Harbor
March 14, 1998

PART I

1974 - 1976

EGREGIOUS

EGREGIOUS was a stock American boat, an Ericson 37, designed to race under the IOR, the rule in use in the 1970's. I had the builders modify her in various ways during construction in 1973. She had no engine, no lifelines, and in a futile effort to prevent potential leaks, no through-hull fittings below the waterline. The head was a bucket; the galley drained into another bucket. Yet her hull cracked at sea and I bailed more than seven tons of water from her every day for months.

The two most significant technological advances in sailing made during the past twenty-five years have been jib-furling gear and Global Positioning Satellite navigation. I had neither aboard EGREGIOUS. GPS did not exist, and jib-furling gear was new and unproven. I rigged EGREGIOUS as a cutter. In the Roaring Forties I sailed her with a working jib and a storm jib set as a staysail. In heavy weather I was able to lower the sails and lash them to the deck, rather than have to make complete sail changes.

I navigated with a secondhand World War II U.S. Navy sextant and time signals obtained from the BBC. Quartz watches were still in the future.

Those who know the word *egregious* are probably familiar with its modern definition, 'flagrantly bad'. A second meaning preceding egalitarianism is 'distinguished or outstanding good'. I chose the name because of its Latin roots, 'out or away from the herd'.

Twenty-five years ago, Cape Horn was more remote than it is today—not of course in distance, but in mind—yet even today more people have climbed Mount Everest than have sailed alone around the Horn. As far as I know I was the first person ever even to try to sail for the Horn alone from California and one of the first to circumnavigate in a modern racing boat. In EGREGIOUS I completed a two-stop solo circumnavigation in what was then world record time, 202 sailing days, breaking the former record of 226 days set by Francis Chichester.

I sought no sponsorship; I hired no public relations agent; I called no press conferences. I did not even notify any breweries, although Guinness somehow heard of the voyage and included me for a while in their book of records. I had not sailed to impress others, but to learn something of the sea and of myself.

During that voyage, as well as more than twelve thousand miles in two earlier unsuccessful attempts, EGREGIOUS, the boat, lived up to both of the antithetical definitions of her name.

---

1 9 7 3
September, took delivery of EGREGIOUS from builder

1 9 7 4
November 2, sailed from San Diego, California for first attempted U.S. solo circumnavigation via Cape Horn
November 21, sustained rigging damage near the Equator; turned downwind toward Tahiti for repairs
December 5, arrived Tahiti
December 23, repairs made, sailed from Tahiti for Cape Horn

1 9 7 5
January 5, rigging again damaged, changed course to return to San Diego for definitive repairs
October 18, again sailed from San Diego for Cape Horn
November 1, hull cracked in gale near the Equator
December 12, became first American to round Cape Horn alone

1 9 7 6
January 21, capsize in Southern Ocean
February 13, strongest wind ever experienced south of Australia
March 5, cyclone in Tasman
March 16, arrived Auckland, New Zealand, after five months at sea
May 7, after repairs, sailed from Auckland for Tahiti
May 26, arrived Tahiti
August 29, sailed from Tahiti for San Diego
October 1, arrived in San Diego, completing two-stop solo circumnavigation in what was then world record time of 202 sailing days

Turning Away

On November 2, 1974, I sailed from San Diego for Cape Horn.

"I was born for this," I wrote, and I believe that I was. Not specifically to sail to Cape Horn—that was a chance of time and timing—but to have sought such a challenge, to have explored whatever the unknown was during my life.

The answer to the question why some people do such things is, like most answers about human behavior, Darwinian, as is that the question is asked in the first place. Most people most of the time seek the safety and stability necessary to perpetuate the species, but the species also needs a few originals—artists and explorers who are radical experiments—in order to adapt. That most such radical experiments end in failure is mathematically certain.

I expected an ordeal. I even wanted an ordeal. If the voyage were easy, someone else would have already made it and I would not learn anything worthwhile. I did not expect the ordeal I had. I did not expect to have to turn away from Cape Horn so soon.

"I am sailing to Tahiti," I wrote sadly in my logbook in the late afternoon of November 21, 1974.

Tahiti has been the South Pacific dream since Captain Cook. It has often been my dream, but it was not then. I was twenty days out of San Diego bound for Cape Horn. And it was strange to sit in the cockpit that evening and sail into the setting sun, when the sun should have been on the starboard beam.

We were at 11°S, 122°W. Cape Horn was four thousand miles to the south and east; Tahiti almost two thousand miles west, completely the wrong direction, but the closest place downwind where I could hope to make repairs to the rudder and the rig.

I concluded the entry, "This is a bitter day."

The sea and solitude were new to me. I was experiencing them with fresh eyes and openness. I had owned and lived on several boats during the preceding six years, and I had made a couple of five hundred mile passages along the Californian and Mexican coasts, one of them nonstop and alone. I was technically a good sailor. I routinely sailed the engineless 37-foot EGREGIOUS in and out of her marina slip and everywhere else. But you do not know the sea until you make long passages offshore. And you do not know solitude until you spend months, and for me ultimately years, alone.

Except for my disappointment, it was not a difficult decision.

The rudder had been grinding and moaning almost from the moment we sailed out of San Diego Bay. It had never made such sounds before, and this bothered me, as did the amount of water I was finding in the bilge of a boat that had no through-hull fittings below the waterline. But those problems would not have caused me to change course.

When you really know a boat, you sail her by feel—the angle of heel, the motion through or off the waves—and, below deck, more than I would have expected, by sound. In later years on other boats, I discovered that I would lose touch with what was happening outside while listening to music in the cabin, which blocked the constant little sounds of hull and water and wind and rig.

The sounds on EGREGIOUS, however, were not subtle.

At about 10:15 the preceding night, I was awakened by a hard, clear metallic crack. I rushed on deck, thinking that some part of the rigging had let go. But when I could not see anything out of place, I discounted the sound and went back to bed.

I had not quite fallen back to sleep when I was startled by a repetition of the same metallic crack. This time I did not have to move from my berth to find the trouble. A few feet away from me the mast was jolting to and fro inside the dark cabin, banging against the deck opening. I lit a kerosene lamp and saw that the two half-inch stainless steel bolts securing the mast to flanges near the overhead were both broken. EGREGIOUS was a stock boat and, as had just been proven, the designer made some engineering errors. Too many yacht designers haven't put in their sea time.

I climbed into the cockpit, disengaged the steering vane, brought the bow through the wind and hove to. My only thought was of how I could steady the mast enough so we could turn back south.

In the dim light of EGREGIOUS's kerosene lamps, I could do little. We remained hove to until dawn, when I sawed some wooden wedges and drove them around the mast. This took several hours, because despite being hove to, we were thrown about considerably by ten-foot waves and forty-knot wind, which was increasing in force. It was 11:00 a.m. before I turned us south again.

Within a few hours, several of the wedges had been pulverized and had to be replaced. After a rest from sawing, I also lashed the mast inside the cabin to the aluminum flanges, which helped, although the line stretched and had to be re-tightened frequently.

With the mast at least momentarily under control, I had time to worry about the bilge again. I had taught myself to sail on San Francisco Bay and had been in gale force winds before, including off California's Point Conception—called 'The Cape Horn of the Pacific Coast', but not by anyone who has been to Cape Horn. This was my first full mid-ocean gale. I simply could not believe that all that water in the bilge was normal. There had to be a leak in the hull. When I unscrewed the liner beneath the sink, I thought I had found it. Water seemed to be seeping under a fiberglass support. Although I couldn't do anything about it, I felt better thinking that at least I knew the source.

I went back up on deck to watch the seas rush toward us. I was admiring the way EGREGIOUS sped through them, when something about the rigging caught my eye. The port lower shroud—the one to windward on the cutter's double-spreader rig—was peculiarly slack. I followed it upward and saw that one of the tangs securing it to the mast was broken. It was a two-part tang, so the shroud had not fallen; but there was no longer any question of driving on for four thousand miles, about half to windward, and then facing Cape Horn. As I watched, the shroud snapped taut. The strain on the remaining half tang was an off-center twist. It could not last long.

We were in an empty part of the ocean. On a traditional trade wind circumnavigation, the longest passage a sailor has to make is the one from North or Central America out to French Polynesia. Many years later, in the Whaling Museum on Nantucket Island, I saw a display about a whaling ship that sank last century near EGREGIOUS's position. All the crew were lost when, for some inexplicable reason, the captain tried to go east in his longboats. South America was closer to him and to me, but it is to windward. After only twenty days, I knew better. So reluctantly I turned toward paradise.

Tahiti is paradise. Not Tahiti itself, which is too developed, although it does still have its charms, but the other Society Islands, particularly Moorea and Bora-Bora. But my spirits were low as we headed west.

The next morning I seriously considered turning around and trying for Valparaiso. I reread the Sailing Directions and pilot charts and recalculated distances. The problem with Tahiti was that it was four thousand miles—two thousand there and two thousand back—in the wrong direction. But I knew that ultimately the problem with Valparaiso—that it was to windward—was greater. There was no chance we could get there without being dismasted.

I had never considered having to put in at Tahiti and had no detailed chart of the area, as I did of Cape Town and Australia, which I had considered likely ports in case of damage. Without any chart other than the general one of the Pacific Ocean, I had to sail almost due west, keeping south of the Marquesas and north of the Tuamotus, also known as the Dangerous Archipelago because they are low islands with unpredictable currents, until I was almost due north of Tahiti and would have clear water to Papeete.

The gale continued for two more days, but the difference between beating and reaching is tremendous. The putative leak was reduced to negligible proportions, which should have told me that in fact there was no leak. Much more water than a sailor expects finds its way into the bilge beating to windward in heavy weather.

The rudder still groaned. Small cracks appeared in the deck around the port side of the mast. The remaining half tang was still to windward, but I had repositioned various halyards and topping lifts and the running backstay, and the strain was significantly reduced.

Before the gale ended I had adapted to the inevitable. I would sail EGREGIOUS to Papeete as quickly as caution permitted, get the boat hauled, do whatever was necessary to the rudder, check the hull, have new tangs and bolts made or sent by air from California, and make another attempt at the Horn, hopefully before the end of the year. Money was a problem. I didn't have much, and Tahiti was reputedly expensive. But I had enough to do what was necessary. I would worry about being broke at the end of the voyage.

When gentle trade winds returned, I even became bored. Ten knots on the beam, low seas, sunshine, was spinnaker weather; but EGREGIOUS limped slowly west under mainsail alone.

There are worse things than being bored. One of them is sprawling in an inflatable dinghy while the stern of your boat rises five feet above you and then falls six feet in a serious effort to impale you on the broken shaft of the self-steering vane. Another is to hammer your thumb rather than the chisel you are using while trying to remove a broken coupling.

One afternoon I was below, napping, secure in the false belief that nothing too bad ever happens on a boat in the daytime, when I felt the mainsail gybe. The entire hull shook. I assumed that perhaps one of the control lines from the self-steering vane to the tiller had broken, but found instead when I went on deck that the servo-rudder was trailing along behind us.

At the moment this did not seem much of a problem. I had a spare coupling aboard, and a spare servo-rudder for that matter. But I soon learned that it was a problem because part of the broken coupling could not, despite my best efforts, be removed from the shaft at sea. Reluctantly accepting the situation, I set the storm jib and ran the sheet aft to the tiller for self-steering. I had experimented with this in San Diego and knew it would work on a broad to a close reach.

The sea was extraordinarily grand the following day, blue-black with white breakers. Small pulls of cloud in the north and east gave way to great masses to the south and west. As I had come to consider usual, the wind blew harder near sunset than it had during the day. We were slicing through the waves at seven to eight knots. Taken in themselves, the past hours could be counted among the reasons I began the voyage. Yet I could not enjoy them. My concern about the mast increased rapidly. Nothing matters aboard a crippled boat except making port.

From within the cabin I sensed the growing wind. A few knots, the spare halyards vibrated. Another knot, the storm jib sheet snapped through the blocks leading it aft to the tiller. I rested my bare foot against the mast and felt it flex with each gust and wondered if each would be the one that would carry it away. Suddenly

9

the storm jib collapsed, blanketed by the mainsail, and we rolled to port instead of starboard. My body tensed as I waited for the shock cords to bring the tiller to leeward before we gybed. A squeak came from the rigging. I stood and stared up through the clear skylight hatch at the mast. The lower shroud looked no worse. But nothing would break slowly. One instant it would be there, and the next, the mast would be gone. I considered reefing the main, but to do so we would have to round up into the wind, which would be harder on the mast than continuing as we were. So we rushed on at eight knots, and I, who love to sail fast, only wished we would slow to six.

Another of our problems—I had become increasingly certain that the hull was not cracked—was solved when the tiller fell off. In another design and/or production failure, the fitting connecting the tiller to the head of the rudder shaft was not up to the task. It bent, wore away bolts, and eventually dropped into the cockpit. Naturally EGREGIOUS gybed, but the wind was not strong and the mast stayed up. I left the cutter hove to while I fitted some spare bolts. They were the same size as the old ones, but the moaning and grinding from the stern never returned.

I taught myself how to navigate, as I did how to sail, and there was negative proof that I knew what I was doing in the absence of land. If my positions were too far off, we would have already run into something. Still we had been out of sight of land for a month and almost five thousand miles, when on December 4, my running fix at noon put us west of Mataiva, the westernmost of the Tuamotus. I hardened up on the sails and turned south for the last three hundred miles to Tahiti. The night was pleasant with a gibbous moon. I spent most of it on deck just in case.

Just before 11:00 a.m. two mornings later a mountain peak rose from the sea off the port bow, precisely where I expected it to be. Under most conditions, Tahiti is an easy landfall. The island is forty miles long and 7,000 feet high and, with its neighbor, Moorea, only seven miles west and itself 4,000 feet high, makes a big target. With the advances in technology, I used my sextant less after my first two circumnavigations. But that moment of my first landfall brought a lasting satisfaction that electronic navigation cannot provide.

I reached the pass through the reef into Papeete just before a spectacular sun set behind Moorea. I followed a local fishing boat through into the lagoon, where some fellow sailors took stern lines ashore and helped me maneuver EGREGIOUS into a Mediterranean-style tie off the Protestant church.

After I got the sails stowed and the lines coiled and ate a can of stew, I pumped up the dinghy, rowed into the harbor, and drifted in the night. I looked back at EGREGIOUS. She was a lovely sight. I hoped, futilely as it turned out, that her troubles were over. I sat quietly, reluctant to return near the land. Automobiles moved on the street along the shore. A dog barked. Some girls sang as they walked past. Papeete even then had a population of 60,000 and was not a quiet place.

I rowed slowly back to the cutter and wandered restlessly. As I passed the compass, I automatically checked the heading, but then realized that there was no need. It was 11:00 p.m. At sea I would have already slept a couple of hours, have already awakened to check the course and wind and speed a couple of times. But now there was no need. No need to go on deck to adjust the shock cords or storm jib sheet for steering, no need to scan the horizon for land or ships. No. I was safe. I, who was to have been rushing toward Cape Horn, was safe in paradise. Perhaps tomorrow I would understand.

2 Eden

The parts needed to repair the damage to EGREGIOUS's rigging and mast finally arrived in Papeete on December 23. I immediately replaced the broken bits, cleared with the port officials, pulled the cutter away from the shore, and let her drift over her anchor, waiting for wind. I was not blind to Tahiti's beauty, but this was not the right time for me to be there. My only passion then was to make another attempt at Cape Horn.

I sat all afternoon. The pass through the reef lay a quarter mile away across a glassy lagoon. The mainsail hung limp. As a cloudy sky darkened into night and I sat in the cockpit eating a can of ravioli, a stranger rowed out from the shore and asked if I wanted to sell the boat. This was odd, for while EGREGIOUS had fallen from grace, I had not expressed any intention of selling her. I laughed and said, "Not today."

After the man left, I remained in the cockpit, watching the lights along the shore and the low clouds clinging to the mountains inland. I was pleased to feel a breeze begin to blow down from those mountains, but less pleased when EGREGIOUS dragged anchor. I had stopped expecting to get to sea that day, but quickly I raised the anchor and hoisted the jib and rode the land breeze down the harbor toward the red and green lights on the buoys marking the pass through the now complete darkness.

As the white line of surf breaking on the reef came closer, our boat speed dropped. EGREGIOUS was on the edge of the land breeze. There was a moment a few hundred yards from the reef when I knew I should turn back and re-anchor. The needle on the knotmeter hovered near three knots—far less than the overly cautious seven recommended for traversing the pass by the pilot book. But a few days earlier I had watched two boats sail through in very light winds, and my desire to resume the voyage was too strong.

Then, just as EGREGIOUS reached the pass, the wind vanished

completely. I tried to turn back, but it was too late. EGREGIOUS would not respond to her helm.

Waves broke only yards to either side. A low swell from the north shook the cutter. Sails slatted uselessly. EGREGIOUS was stalled right in the middle of the pass. The wind must return, I told myself, as though my wishes meant anything. The buoy to starboard was farther away than it had been a moment before. EGREGIOUS began to drift helplessly down onto the reef to the west.

I have compared sailing an engineless boat to performing on a trapeze without a safety net. You cannot afford to make a mistake. Yet I had made a mistake. It wasn't in refusing to have an engine, for I later sailed through that pass even on a boat with an engine. My mistake was in letting impatience and a dragging anchor dictate my departure.

Nothing I did made any difference. EGREGIOUS was so close that an anchor would not keep us off. My only hope was that we would somehow bounce across the coral without breaking up. My last thought before I expected to be caught by the breakers was that I should have sold the boat to the man who had rowed out an hour earlier.

EGREGIOUS was there. The bow was in the line of white foam. Simultaneously, I felt the faintest breath of wind. EGREGIOUS responded to the tiller, but I was afraid it was too late. I tried not to oversteer, careful not to diminish our almost imperceptible headway. Slowly, painfully slowly, we ghosted away.

I spent Christmas day repairing a torn seam in the mainsail while EGREGIOUS pressed south under jib and staysail.

We passed Raivavae Island, the last land I could expect to see before the distant Horn. And then, partially because of the truly open sea ahead of us, partially because of the relief at escaping from the hassles in Tahiti, partially because I was again heading toward the Horn and the prospect of fulfilling a twenty-year long dream, perhaps partially because, unable to afford to do much reprovisioning at Papeete prices, I was not eating enough, I began to enter an almost mystical mental state.

On December 29, I noted in the log that despite being hard on thirty-knot southeast trade winds, "My sense of well-being is immense. I truly love sailing and am grateful for these last few hours." On December 30, it was: "Today is the finest of the voyage so far. I do not know exactly why I feel that, because it has not been exceptional in any way. We are sailing smoothly and well. I have a sense of space and openness and solitude in this Southern Ocean that I have not known before. I love the idea of the empty sea before me. Sail on, EGREGIOUS, sail on."

On New Year's Day I wrote, "I have been reading and lean back and close my eyes and listen to the water gurgle past the hull, the splash of the bow wave. I breathe deeply and am filled with peace. I have earned this peace, and I welcome it."

And then on January 3 and 4, as I entered the Roaring Forties for the first time, the experience peaked.

"I believe that I am an articulate man, but this is not an experience to be articulated. No nouns, no verbs suffice. There is the sea, but it is unremarkable just now. There is the wind, light and backing toward the north. There is the sky, covered by a layer of low, fuzzy clouds. There is the cutter sailing smoothly southeast. Nothing is exceptional other than the overwhelming sense of peace, which has increased day by day and is now absolute. I have never been so calm and content. I am always hungry, yet that only renders my senses more acute. A sailor is an artist whose medium is the wind. But now I feel the wind more sensitively than ever before. It touches my face, blows over my skin, enters my body, more essential than blood. At this moment I want for nothing. I am whole, complete, one, transcendent. Yet I am also transcended and do not exist except as a part of the beauty around me. The sea is steel blue and the sky light gray. On the western horizon, a single pale yellow band lingers behind the already-set sun. Although it is dusk, there is a sense of dawn, of expectancy. This is a view of Eden, of what the world must have been like the first day after creation."

The next morning I awoke to a storm—the light backing wind had been a warning—that soon broke the tangs and bolts replaced in Tahiti. The mystical state was replaced by depression. Cape Horn, instead of being less than a month ahead, receded to the infinite perspective of the unassailable.

3 Cape Horn

After limping all the way back to San Diego, five thousand miles north, with spare halyards and topping lifts and running backstays shifted to support the port side of the mast, under severely reduced sail, setting only the storm jib as a headsail and in all but the lightest wind reefing the main, EGREGIOUS was extensively repaired.

One of the things I had learned about myself was that my commitment was absolute. On October 18, 1975 I sailed for Cape Horn again.

Although I wore gloves, my hands turned blue when I bailed. There was no doubt the hull was cracked: I had gone over the side during a lull a few weeks and several thousand miles earlier and located the hairline running up the trailing edge of the keel.

Even while sleeping I wore long underwear, wool pants, four shirts, two pairs of socks, a watch cap, and still I was cold. When I first got up in the morning, my fingers were swollen twice their normal size, the skin drum taut, like sausages. It was December. Summertime in the Southern Ocean. The sun was about as far south as it would ever get. The temperature of both air and water were just above freezing, about as warm as they would ever get. For the third successive day there was sleet and snow. Somehow I had not thought to bring a shovel, so I was grateful when waves washed the snow from the cockpit.

I was not complaining. I was precisely where I wanted to be. Through years and women and waves and wanton storms that raged without and within, I had kept coming at Cape Horn. And at last, on my third attempt, it was very near. How near I did not know because I had not had a sextant sight for several days, but near. A few hundred miles ahead.

The sea was a symphony of violence. Each day the barometer moved at least half an inch. Crests were blown from twenty-foot waves; spindrift was everywhere. Never before had the sea seemed so alive. That it isn't was brought home to me by one of the great wandering albatross, that, in those big waves, I often saw gliding in troughs below me. This one soared beside EGREGIOUS for several seconds and then turned his head and looked at me deliberately. Eye held eye. Life acknowledged life.

One morning I was on the foredeck lowering the staysail, when I happened to glance down just as a wave passed. While in fact it was moving forward and EGREGIOUS was sliding down its back, the momentary sensation was that the boat was going forward, about to take a two-story drop. It was a long way down.

Every once in a while, a set of bigger waves, perhaps twenty to thirty feet, went through.

I was standing in the companionway, having just lifted a bucket full of ice water from the bilge, when I saw a line of immense curling crests speeding toward me. In retrospect I should have closed the hatch, but I was mesmerized. The crest of the last giant toppled ten yards to windward, and I thought we would be inundated; but EGREGIOUS, despite her imperfections, had many virtues, and she turned her hip and rose gracefully through seething foam.

After fifty days and six thousand miles of sailing south, our course was now east. My later advice to anyone wanting to sail from California to Cape Horn was simple: sail south until the rigging freezes over and turn left. We had made that turn. Odd that a compass course could bring such joy.

I let my mind race ahead. East to the Horn. East, east, east, with the soaring albatrosses and the petrels and the shearwaters and prions. East fleeing before the shrieking gales, running with the foaming waves. East across the South Atlantic, across the Southern Ocean. East past Africa. Past Australia, past Tasmania and the Tasman Sea. East with the hissing, driving spray. East toward the rising sun. East, east, east past New Zealand. East halfway across the Pacific. East for twelve thousand miles. East for days and weeks and months. East until finally at long last we could turn north and leave the Forties behind and perhaps be warm again. That was the plan; but I knew it would not happen that way. Somewhere I would have to put in to repair the hull. I did not care. We would have already rounded Cape Horn.

Back in California I knew that some people were thinking about me, wondering where I was at that moment, what I was doing. If they guessed either bailing or re-stitching the mainsail, they would have a 90% probability of being right. The sails were top quality, but they were not heavy enough, particularly the main. For this the sailmaker was not entirely to blame. No one had ever before sailed alone from California for Cape Horn, so no one really knew how strong the sails must be. I spent a lot of time sewing. The mainsail had to be lowered and dragged into the cabin three of the first five days south of 50°S. And when the wind went east for a few hours, I did not drive EGREGIOUS hard to windward to save both the hull and the sails.

The wind was less constant than I expected, blowing fifteen, then thirty, fifteen, then thirty, making it difficult to adjust the Aries steering vane, and causing EGREGIOUS to yaw between a heading of 90° and 160°. The only constants were that every day became colder and every day passed without my being able to get a sun sight. The two were related. Without sights to fix our position, the safest course was to go further south, which made it colder.

On December 11, I decided that we must be south of the Horn, and set the steering vane to a course that I hoped would average due east. My dead reckoning put us on the latitude of the Diego Ramirez Islands, some fifty miles southwest of the cape. If I saw them and conditions were favorable, I would close Horn Island. If not, I would pass it unseen.

Each morning, with only rare exceptions imposed by the weather, I baked biscuits. Usually I just dropped lumps of dough on the pan—after all they tasted as good no matter what the shape—but perhaps partly to demonstrate to myself that I could still impose order on chaos, I decided to make proper biscuit-shaped biscuits that morning. I dug out the cookie cutter and carefully formed six beautiful biscuits. However, no sooner had I put them in to bake, when I realized that something extraordinary was occurring outside: the sun was casting shadows.

Without taking the time for foulweather gear, I grabbed the stopwatch and sextant and dashed on deck, climbing to the stern where I could sometimes see the sun from behind the mainsail and through the clouds. But EGREGIOUS was rolling so much, the horizon so broken by leaping waves, the sun so dim, that I could not manage a useful sight.

After fifteen minutes of futile effort, I smelled something burning. As I started forward, a freezing wave broke over me.

I rescued the biscuits and set them on the galley counter, while I dried myself and the sextant. Before I finished, another wave struck EGREGIOUS abeam, and all but one of the biscuits fell into the bilge.

At noon the day improved sufficiently so that I was able to get my first good sun sights for five days. Unless I was making some serious error in calculation, the Diego Ramirez Islands were not far ahead.

I spent most of the afternoon bundled in many layers of clothes and foulweather gear, sitting in the companionway, staring ahead. The sun disappeared behind thickening clouds, and at intervals sleet drove me below decks. At 4:46 p.m. I had just heated some spaghetti and returned to sit in the companionway to eat, when I looked up and saw land. The first land since Guadalupe Island two days out of San Diego. For weeks I had sailed across the great bands of weather: the northeast trades, the doldrums, the southeast trades, the horse latitudes, the Roaring Forties; I had marked little x's on charts; I had told myself that I was nearing Cape Horn; but I had dreamed and struggled for so long that it did not seem real until I saw those desolate rocks ahead. Now, even if the mast came down, EGREGIOUS would be blown past the Horn.

A little more than two hours later the cutter passed south of the southernmost of the Diego Ramirez Islands. The wind was only twenty-five knots, but the surf against the green-gray cliffs was impressive. Cape Horn tomorrow, I kept telling myself. I could hardly believe it. But it was true.

That night the Horn lived up to its reputation. The wind increased quickly to a gale. By dawn it was blowing fifty knots, and during the day it built to a full Force 12. Long before it reached that strength, the mainsail ripped. I manhandled it into the cabin and re-stitched the torn seam, but I didn't attempt the by then impossible task of resetting the sail.

The waves increased again to twenty to thirty feet now that EGREGIOUS was sailing over the shallow continental shelf, and there were two sets, one coming from the southwest, driven before the gale; the other from the northwest, rebounding from the land. Both sets of waves were breaking.

For the first time, and one of only a handful ever, I tied myself in the cockpit to steer.

Averaging eight knots under bare poles, EGREGIOUS rolled from beam to beam, sometimes in those cross seas rolling to port, sometimes to starboard. Even though it was not in operation, the servo-rudder for the Aries remained in the water, and as EGREGIOUS surfed down some of the larger waves, a rooster tail rose from it, as from a hydroplane. The strain on the tiller was immense, often forcing me to brace myself with my legs and use both arms to drag the cutter back on course. There was no time to turn to see on which quarter the next dangerous wave loomed, but after a while I knew by feel and sound. And though I caught only glimpses of them as they swooped across my field of vision, even in the strongest wind albatrosses and petrels soared about as usual.

Through what was a very long day, I steered. Finally, at 7:00 p.m. the wind decreased to thirty knots, and I was able to engage the Aries. Stiff and cold and tired and hungry, I stumbled into the cabin.

After cooking a victory banquet of canned stew, I put a Bach fugue on the cassette player. Bach's music was a small but triumphant sound there at 57°S.

I knew that I had just become the first American to round Cape Horn alone; but even if I had not been the first, the struggle would have been worthwhile and the day should have been as hard as it was. A smashed hand, frostbite, piercing cold, fatigue were all made endurable. The water I bailed from the bilge into the Atlantic that morning had come from the Pacific the night before. Cape Horn, which a year earlier had seemed so impossibly remote, was behind me.

Capsize

There is a myth perpetuated by people musing over globes in dry rooms ashore and public relations agents for the round-the-world races that great waves roll unimpeded around the world in high southern latitudes. One of the troubles with public relations hype is that it exaggerates when the truth is sufficient.

As everyone since Captain Cook who has ever actually sailed the Southern Ocean knows, waves there, as everywhere else, rise and fall with pressure systems. Two days after the Force 12 wind off Cape Horn, EGREGIOUS sat becalmed on a flat and glassy sea while an albatross swam circles around her, looking for a handout.

When the wind returned, EGREGIOUS continued east through two fogs: one a small cold circle of visibility barely extending beyond her bow; the other the fog of Chancery Court in Dickens *Bleak House*, which I was reading.

The crack in the hull seemed manageable. Wanting to get as far as I could during the southern summer, I did not divert to the Falklands or Cape Town. By mid-January I was about halfway between Africa and Australia, at a latitude varying a few degrees either side of 45°S.

January 22, 1976

I don't know how long I'll be able to write. I do not feel well at all. Blood and kerosene are all over the cabin. I have a broken stove, a hopelessly shredded storm jib, and a smashed face—our second capsize in fourteen hours came at 5:15 a.m., bashing me above the right eye with a drawer full of books. This is the most dangerous storm I have been in thus far. The broken stove bothers me as much as anything. Cold food from now on? Perhaps I have a concussion. I'm too dizzy to write more.

January 23

Today I have a black eye—more precisely a vivid magenta eye—from which I cannot see clearly, a severe headache, continued dizziness, a desperate need for a storm jib, and as desperate a longing to be in port with the voyage successfully completed.

The barometer rose rapidly last evening and as rapidly fell, with fifty-knot winds returning near dawn. I lowered the jib, and we drifted ahull for five hours. Then, although the barometer continued to fall, so did the wind, and we resumed sailing. Now, at 3:00 p.m. we run at eight knots before a near-gale.

I will try to go back and make some sense of these past few days, but they are very jumbled in my mind. From now on any errors in judgment or navigation can be blamed on brain damage.

The afternoon of January 20 was so sunny and warm that I washed my body for the first time this year and then sunbathed in the cockpit.

I once read that the mountain men of the American West used to sew themselves in their long underwear in the fall and not take it off until spring. Perhaps that is only a legend. But when I removed the long underwear I put on two months and an ocean earlier and threw it overboard, it was so strong that it did not sink and when last seen was walking briskly toward the South Pole.

Increasing wind in the evening led me to put on my other set of long underwear and lower the mainsail about 7:00 p.m.

As soon as the mainsail was down, I almost re-raised it because our speed dropped below six knots. However, I decided to leave the sail down and make another evaluation later. By the time I went to sleep at midnight, there was no doubt that the jib alone was enough. We were doing a solid seven knots under a cloudy night sky.

At 2:00 a.m. I awakened to feel EGREGIOUS heeling over farther and ever farther. There was no special noise; we were rushing smoothly through the water, pressed over on our beam. I waited for the boat to rise back to a more normal angle, but she did not. She simply stayed there. No fuss. The sail was not flogging. We were not pounding. There was no particular sound of wind, only hissing water outside the hull. And still she did not come up.

I pulled myself from my bunk, donned clothes, foulweather gear, safety harness, and climbed on deck, while we continued steadily on, sailing heeled 70°.

On deck, the sensation of speed and the force of the wind were awesome. Everything seemed quiet inside the cabin because a fifty-knot wind came up so quickly that there were no seas.

I crawled forward on the inclined deck as one would crawl along the face of a mountain. It was a solid wind, a wind to lean against—indeed a wind that had to be leaned against.

Because it is easier to lower the jib when it is partially blanketed by the storm jib/staysail, I attempted to raise that sail first, but was unable to free one of its lashings. I wedged my feet onto the toerail, held onto the forestay with one hand, and fumbled with the knot with the other; all the time in a standing position, face to the deck, feet only inches above the water.

Finally the storm jib was free, and I raised it and lowered the jib. EGREGIOUS rose from her side and that was all for the night.

The leak in the hull is never more irritating than in the morning after a night of heavy weather. The water splashing about makes the cabin sound like the inside of a washing machine. When I got up to bring some order to that chaos, the barometer was low and steady. Not until early afternoon did conditions deteriorate.

I fell asleep sitting in my berth reading and was again awakened suddenly, this time by waves breaking over us. The compass by the chart table revealed that we had spun 90° off course and were sailing directly south. I decided I had better steer.

For the fourth time so far on this passage, the wind was gusting to sixty knots, and the waves averaging twenty feet. But these waves were steeper, more concave, and more violent than any I had yet seen.

During most of the afternoon the sun continued to shine between fluffy low clouds, and the temperature was not uncomfortable. I was able to keep us headed east, and our speed averaged about seven knots under the storm jib alone, although often we exceeded ten while surfing down crests. At 3:30 I thought it would be safe for me to go below for something to eat.

About a minute after I got into the cabin, just as I was opening a galley locker, we were turned upside down by a wave, with the mast perhaps 70° below the water. I felt the wave coming, but did not expect it to be any worse than many that had already skipped us like a stone across the ocean. I reached out to brace myself against the companionway ladder. Wasted effort. I flew, or more accurately dropped, down through the cabin against what is designated the overhead but which was peculiarly below me, finally coming to rest in a corner near the chart table, accompanied by pans, plastic canisters, packages of food, eating utensils, water containers, cups, books, and four guaranteed unbreakable plates, one of which fragmented into hundreds of tiny slivers. The lid came off a jar of sugar, liberally coating everything with sticky saltwater syrup.

In the main part of the cabin, a hundred books were thrown above the restraining rail on the starboard bookshelf across to the upper berth on the opposite side of the cabin. As were various articles of clothing, a compass, and my Zenith Transoceanic radio, essential for precise time signals needed for celestial navigation. These, too, ended on the upper port berth, having seconds before been on the upper starboard one. Nothing fell into the center of the cabin. We were so far over, their trajectories followed mine, ricocheting against the overhead before fetching up to port as EGREGIOUS's eight-thousand-pound keel quickly pulled us back upright without our doing a full 360°. Once the boat is that far over, it does not make much difference which side she comes back up just so long as she does.

Fortunately, I had closed the companionway behind me, but considerable ocean still managed to find its way into the cabin. I opened the hatch and looked out. The cockpit was full of water, and the plywood windvane on the self-steering gear was missing. With no control on the helm, we were pointing into the wind. The storm jib was slatting horribly, shaking the mast and rig as if determined to tear EGREGIOUS apart. I did not seem to be injured, although later my left wrist swelled painfully. Before I could restore order to the cabin, I had to do something about the steering.

Not having removed my foulweather gear, I was able to go immediately on deck and take the tiller. A stray line blocked one of the drains, so water subsided only very slowly from EGREGIOUS's large cockpit. Even with the additional weight aft, she rose easily to the confused seas. A boat to be loved as well as hated.

Although I needed to be in several places at once, I had no choice but to remain at the tiller until the cockpit finally emptied.

Then I managed to find and fit a spare vane and go below to attempt to bail out the cabin.

As I bailed, wave after wave broke over us, sending more and more water cascading in. I stopped, closed the companionway, and waited for a lull. Then I threw another bucketful into the cockpit—there was no time to send it over the side—and another wave came aboard and below. Not until late afternoon was I able to lift one last bucket from an almost empty bilge, and then re-stow all the debris that had come loose and pick up all the slivers of glass I could find.

During all of this, the sun continued to shine merrily on hard black waves, and the barometer, while low, remained steady, as it did for the remainder of that evening.

When I got up to bail at 3:00 a.m. we were sailing southeast at seven knots, the wind and waves were still powerful but definitely not as strong as earlier and the barometer was rising rapidly. The bilge seemed fuller than usual, but I would have to wait for better weather to know if the leak was worse. All the indications were that the storm was passing. I fell into my first real sleep for nights.

Two hours later I was awakened from that sleep by a violent blow in the face as we again capsized. It seemed to take EGREGIOUS longer to right herself than before. I knew instantly what had happened, but was trapped in the tangle of my sleeping bag. I was pinned not in my berth, but between the railing on the upper berth and the aluminum side support to the mast. As the keel swung back into the sea, I slid down the back rest to the lower berth. A drawer of oversized books which had flown across the cabin and hit me in the face fell onto the cabin sole. One of those books was Adlard Coles' *Heavy Weather Sailing*. Being clobbered by his book was a hazard of the sea he had not warned against.

Blood ran into my mouth and onto the sodden sleeping bag. I noticed that my pillow was gone, and for some reason it seemed important that I find it; but I could not do so. Much later I found it beneath a sail bag in the forepeak. I touched my nose and forehead hesitantly with fingers which came away covered with blood. As I looked at them, I thought, "Of course they're bloody. What did you expect, you fool?" and with that I struggled from the sleeping bag.

My reflection in a shard of mirror showed a skinned nose and a two-inch gash diagonally across my right eyebrow. But as I was inspecting these wounds, it was obvious that something more urgent was wrong outside.

That we should be thrown off course was to be expected, and the compass by the chart table showed us heading northwest. I thought the self-steering vane had broken again, but a glance aft found it intact. But we did not come back on course and the storm jib continued to flail about. It had been torn in two and the corner to which the sheets were attached trailed twenty feet behind the stern. The remnant of the sail still hanked onto the forestay had split into two more pieces.

Without a storm jib I had no choice but to lie ahull, which we did throughout the morning, while I repeated the drill of cleaning up the cabin and then tried to repair the stove, which failed to light. The kerosene fuel tank leaked and would not hold pressure. Whether this was caused by the capsizes or was a coincidence of timing I did not know. To have to face the Southern Ocean without hot food—not even a cup of coffee—was extremely disheartening.

I worked on the stove for hours, spreading soot and kerosene everywhere and accomplishing nothing more than making myself vomit. I don't know if this was due to the smell of kerosene combined with EGREGIOUS's spastic motion or a symptom of concussion.

The stove is definitely useless for the duration. Much of my food cannot be eaten uncooked, and the rest is unpalatable. Cold hash will be like eating dog food. I can find enough to stay alive, but what an additional misery. I tried heating water over the kerosene cabin light. After a twenty minute ballet, it became lukewarm.

The wind continues to build. Without a storm jib, my choices are to carry on under the jib, even though at present it is too much sail, or lie ahull. At this moment we are sailing, but with any further increase in wind, I will lie ahull.

The sun was briefly visible late this morning and I got a sight which puts us at 43°44′ S, but have to guess at the longitude. Dead reckoning is too dignified a designation for my estimates of our position these last three days. However I believe we are near 63° E, the antipodes of San Diego. Africa is two thousand miles behind; Australia two thousand miles ahead. Being halfway around the world should be cause for celebration, but somehow I don't feel up to it. Only two days ago I thought we were not doing too badly.

January 24

Darkness. Darkness of the alien nights in harbor. Darkness of the eerie sail in zero visibility in the probable proximity to icebergs in the South Atlantic. The terrible darkness of the spirit when I had to turn away from the Horn on my first attempts. And now the silent darkness of fear as I lie in my bunk and wait.

I do not know the time, but it could not yet be midnight. I lay down about 9:00 p.m. The water in the bilge is not yet too noisy. EGRE-GIOUS is lying ahull under bare poles. Outside the storm has entered a fierce ecstasy, but my main impression from inside the cabin is of quiet. I hate lying ahull. On another boat I once steered for thirty-three out of thirty-six hours. I cannot afford that exhaustion yet. And I cannot get any sail on her; it is physically impossible. I have tried.

Several times this storm has deceived me into believing it to be abating. Until tonight, despite the capsizes, it had not been worse than weather we have experienced three or four times before. The capsizes were not caused by exceptionally big waves, but by particularly steep and concave ones. Now the storm is fulfilling its destiny. I am certain the wind is more than sixty knots, but I have no idea how much more.

After writing this afternoon and eating a dinner of cold canned ham and beans, I went on deck to decide if I should lower the jib. For almost an hour I sat in the cockpit, until something urgently told me to get the sail down. No sooner had I let the halyard run than EGREGIOUS was knocked down by a blast from the south. I clung to the mast; then when she came back up, I made my way to the bow to lash the jib. While there, I had another presentiment of danger and grabbed the headstay with both hands just as a wave crashed over me. EGREGIOUS was again knocked down, and I washed overboard, suspended in space and water until she struggled once again to her feet and I swung back aboard. My safety harness was clipped on, but I am grateful not to have put it to the test. My religious friends no doubt are certain that an angel watches over me at such moments, but if so, it had better have the wings of an albatross.

We are heeled 20° from the force of the wind against the mast. The howling seems distant. Then a wave hits, sometimes with a crack like a rifle shot, sometimes with a hollow thud, sometimes with a warning roar of foam, sometimes with no warning at all. We heel farther and farther over; the hull groans and crackles; we are pushed and driven and slammed down against the stone-hard sea. I do not know how much more EGREGIOUS can take; I do not know why one of these waves has not already found her wound and split us wide open. Not since Papeete Pass do I recall being this afraid at sea. I know I am projecting that fear into the elements, but this storm seems relentless, sinister, vindictive. Rain pounds against the deck. Three huge waves hit us in rapid succession. Somehow EGREGIOUS lurches back from each. There is a lull, and I drift into an uneasy sleep.

I have been reading a biography of Clarence Darrow—or rather, I was ages ago when I had time to read—and as I sleep I dream I am a lawyer in a courtroom. I stand and say "Your Honor," and the courtroom lurches and I am thrown back into my chair. I stand again. "Your Honor." The room lurches and I fall. That is all there is to the dream: the endless repetition of my standing, the words "Your Honor," a lurch, and a fall.

I am awakened by another onslaught of waves. Through the hatch I see the sky is still dark, so it cannot yet be 4:00 a.m. The water in the bilge is wild, obscuring even the breaking waves and the roar of the wind. I hate the leak, hate having to pull myself from my berth, dress and bail in the middle of the night, hate listening in an effort to determine if it has grown worse, hate wondering if it will kill me.

For navigation my watch is set to Greenwich time. 23:00 GMT. 3:00 a.m. here. The barometer which rose 1/2 inch and then dropped 1 inch has risen 1/10 inch. Wonderful.

I open the hatch and am met by an undiminished blast of wind and rain. Mechanically I begin to bail. My probably-sprained left wrist prevents me from lifting a full bucket. Half buckets obviously mean I take twice as long, probably more, because there is more opportunity for waves and rain to come below.

I return to my bunk and try to sleep.

January 25

The storm is finally and truly over. Last night the bolt connecting the tiller to the rudder post broke again. I replaced it again.

We are sailing east under main and jib.

5 *The Incomparable Wind*

Three weeks and more than two thousand miles east of the Southern Ocean storm, I was south of Australia, still in the Roaring Forties.

Between when I bailed at 2:00 a.m and when I bailed at 4:30 a.m. on February 13, the barometer began a steep decline—a decline which carried it into virgin territory far below any previous reading in my experience. This was to be a day far beyond my experience.

With that precipitous drop, still there came no increase in wind. EGREGIOUS continued boisterously but safely east, while I searched the dawn sky in vain for signs of the apocalypse. I returned to my berth but did not undress or try to sleep.

Every half hour I got up. The barometer quickened its downward acceleration; EGREGIOUS continued her fine sail; I continued to become ever more anxious. Something incredible and probably terrible was happening, but the only sign was the barometer.

There was no point in trying to rest. I donned my foulweather gear and stood in the galley, drinking air temperature instant coffee, which means cold coffee, and looking out at the sea and waiting.

When at 7:30 a.m. conditions began to change, they changed rapidly. Within a few minutes, the wind increased to forty knots, and I lowered the jib and raised the storm jib. A few minutes later, I lowered the storm jib. And then the wind went off the scale.

Just before it struck, I finished tying myself in the cockpit. At one moment, everything was under control, EGREGIOUS moving safely along at five knots under bare poles; then the tiller was wrenched from my hands and slammed against the starboard cockpit seat. I remember being glad I had lowered the storm jib in time. No sail, much less one repaired as often as that one, could have stood such a blast. EGREGIOUS careened to port, broadside to a wind far beyond any I had imagined, a wind that leveled everything before it, a wind that pressed us down into the sea until I began to fear we would be forced under.

There were no waves. The wind flatted the sea. Using all my strength, I fought Egregious's bow back downwind. We were making nine to ten knots under bare poles; not surfing, just being inexorably forced ahead. It was like sailing through fog. I could not see the compass two feet away. Yet there was no fog. The wind tore the surface from the sea and flailed it about my eyes. I breathed cautiously, trying to inhale more air than salt water. I like to believe I am inner-directed, but I thought, "This is too much, simply too much. It is too bad no one will know I got this far, that I rounded the Horn before I was killed."

When it struck, I had no way of knowing how long it would last, but I did know that I was at the tiller for the duration. This was the time to steer beyond exhaustion. Fortunately that incomparable wind passed within an hour, leaving us to lie ahull gratefully to a fifty-knot gale, which by comparison was a relief.

At 3:30 a.m. the next morning I was able to set the storm jib, only to discover that the self-steering gear was broken—more than broken—dismembered. Nothing in so exposed a position could have endured.

I was able to rig sheet to tiller self-steering and we continued east, limping a bit more from each blow.

In the last light of sunset, I noted in my log:

"Had I written this earlier today, I would have said how tired I am of the constant battle, tired of shackles that won't open, tired of halyards that foul aloft, tired of being constantly wet and cold, tired of lying ahull, tired of being in pain every time I put on my sea boots, tired of the terrible weather.

"On the radio I hear that we have encountered an exceptionally bad southern summer. Australia is experiencing devastating storms and floods, New Zealand record rainfall, and Egregious many, many more days of gales than to be expected on average; including, according to the pilot chart, a zero probability of gales at our present position. I am tired of knots that jam, and most of all I am tired of the leak, or rather the sound of the leak.

"That is what I would have written this morning and it is all true; but today was so fine with blue sky and sea and a steady if cold wind, that it revived me. I am pleased just to be alive today and know that I have subjected myself of my own free will to all those things of which I am tired. Nevertheless, for a hot shower and an uninterrupted night's sleep, I would gladly sell my somewhat-tarnished soul. The Devil is never around when you really want him."

Repeatedly during my first circumnavigation I called winds or waves or storms "the worst I have ever seen" and then I would experience something that would redefine 'worst'.

The wind on that February day, however, was incomparable. It was the strongest wind I had been in then; and, more than twenty years and three circumnavigations later, it is still the strongest wind I have ever been in.

It came from an incredibly tight, dense, and, thankfully, small low. A barograph would have shown an almost perfectly symmetrical funnel: a long, gradual decline, a precipitous drop, a minute base, followed by a rapid climb, then a continued gradual rise. Had the center of the storm been any larger, had it lasted for twenty hours or even ten or had there been a lee shore, survival for any small boat would have been unlikely.

New Zealand meteorological records verified that in Cyclone Colin I experienced sustained seventy-knot winds with higher gusts. For that hour on February 13, the wind was much stronger than Colin's highest gust. How much higher I cannot say beyond that it was at least twenty to thirty knots higher, so conservatively it was at least ninety to one hundred knots. Perhaps more. Incomparable is incomparable.

Every once in a while I read of someone's 'storm management' techniques. This is the greatest conceit since we named ourselves *homo sapiens* and only provides further superfluous proof that we are *homo insipiens*.

Small storms you manage. Big ones you merely hope to outlive.

6 Cyclone in the Tasman

On February 20, when Southwest Cape, Tasmania, was visible purple against a pale rose sky moments before the sun emerged dripping from the sea, I saw land for the first time since the Diego Ramirez Islands the preceding December 11.

Becalmed a few hours later off the temporarily misnamed 'Storm Bay', I knew that EGREGIOUS could not survive another month in the Southern Ocean and that I must take advantage of the repair facilities in Australia or New Zealand.

When the wind returned, I changed course north.

On February 28, I crossed 40°S and left the Roaring Forties and Fifties, which I had entered November 26, 1975. I thought I was passing into safer waters.

"Ninety-eight. Ninety-nine. One hundred." I counted to myself and then stopped to rest. The numbers were buckets of water I was bailing from the bilge of EGREGIOUS, lying ahull in the Tasman Sea on March 5, my 140th consecutive day at sea. I had continued sailing as long as possible. Now perhaps I had gone too far.

It was 3:00 a.m. With a few more buckets the bilge would be as empty as it ever got now that the sea inexorably entered at seventy to eighty gallons each hour. Outside the dark cabin the wind was hideous. Halyards clanged against the mast like fire alarms; banshees wailed through the rigging; rain rattled against the deck; and every evil, frightful spirit from the nightmares of childhood screamed and shrieked. The waves were twenty feet high and with that peculiar steep concave form which had twice capsized us more than a month earlier. There could no longer be any doubt. This gale had become a cyclone.

The capsize I feared came moments after I returned to bed. Three huge waves struck us in rapid succession. The first two knocked us down; the third rolled EGREGIOUS over to port. For a moment I hoped it would not be more than a knockdown, but then the mast went beneath the water and all the objects which seemed impossible to dislodge fell through the cabin, even though in preparation for just such an eventuality I had carefully re-stowed everything only hours before. Plates, pans, cans, cutlery, books, pillows, soggy sleeping bags and myself congregated on what was usually designated the overhead, but which at the moment was not. I was beginning to think EGREGIOUS was more watertight upside down than right side up. Then the eight-thousand-pound keel pulled us back, and I struggled from the mess that tried to bury me in my berth.

My first step was to the bilge. With every blow from every wave I had been fearing EGREGIOUS would split open. Now as I stared down into a bilge overflowing again with water, I thought it had happened. The Tasman was a sea too far. We were finally going down.

Hope and heroism did not enter into my actions. I struggled out of habit and because there was nothing else to do. The dinghy had long been half inflated and the supplies I would take with me collected into sailbags: food, water, solar stills, navigation equipment, clothing, foulweather gear, hat, rigging knife, can openers, utensils, buckets, vitamin pills, sunburn lotion, passport, money. But I could never abandon ship in these seventy-knot winds. The dinghy would be blown away the instant I got it on deck.

So I began to bail, using the same methodical pace as when I bailed after the last capsize, a pace perfected during the intervening weeks when I came to be bailing eight hours out of every twenty-four, never sleeping for more than forty-five minutes before being awakened by the ocean splashing over the cabin sole, and during the day, reading a chapter of a book and then bailing, reading a chapter, then bailing. A slow reader would drown that way. Water weighs about 8 1/2 pounds a gallon and I was lifting more than one thousand five hundred gallons, seven tons, each day.

I did not think as I bent and dipped the bucket into the depths of the hull, or as I braced myself against the onslaught of subsequent waves, or as I threw the water out into the cockpit. There were no visions of the pleasures of life I would never know. There was not even any regret. There was no fear. Perhaps I was too near exhaustion, but I did not feel tired. Truly I was resigned. Bucket after bucket, gallon after gallon, made no appreciable difference. I knew I had made a mistake. Beyond EGREGIOUS's every weakness, these moments were of my own making. Bend, dip, lift, throw. Bend, dip, lift, throw. I could have made many ports. Cape Town. Perth. Melbourne. Hobart. Sydney. But then if I had not persisted I would never have kept going for the Horn after the two earlier attempts failed. The ancient Greek concept of the tragic flaw: My strength had become the instrument of my destruction. Bend, dip, lift, throw.

I did not think I could keep us afloat, only that I would try to do so as long as possible, that I must continue to total exhaustion, that I must go to my limit as well as EGREGIOUS's. Bend, dip, lift, throw. Part of me was detached, aloof, watching myself as I worked mutely. Often I had wondered what my last word would be if I were lost during the voyage, but now I knew there would be none. My silence and I were inseparable. Bend, dip, lift, throw. I had been bailing a long time: I had no idea how long, but the sky seemed less dark, and oddly the longer I bailed, the less tired I became.

Dawn revealed a leaden sky, twenty- to thirty-foot seething waves, and that I was gaining on the leak. I was actually disappointed. This must be carefully explained. I adamantly did not want to die, but thinking—no, knowing I soon would—had the unexpected effect of filling me with life. I was bursting with it. I was euphoric. I could bail forever. Everything was so simple: I bail. That was all. There was absolutely nothing else. Nothing at all. I was very happy. Bend, dip, lift, throw. I would have bailed as the water rose above my knees. I would have climbed the companionway steps and bailed when it reached my waist. Absurdly, I would have bailed as EGREGIOUS lay awash an instant before she sank and I would have known it to be absurd but I would have bailed anyway. And now I will not have to. Life drains from me as I drain the sea from the bilge, and is replaced by unutterable fatigue.

I would have liked to have slept for days, but in an hour I was up again bailing. It is in the nature of a long solo sailing passage that one must continue to struggle far beyond what one would have thought to be ultimate limits. EGREGIOUS had for the moment survived, but she was no longer a sailing vessel. She had become a derelict to be nursed to the nearest refuge—Auckland, if we could make it, but the west coast of New Zealand's North Island if necessary. The sea had become her unnatural element.

For nine days I had been unable to get any sights to fix our position and two more would pass before I would verify that we were four hundred miles southwest of the nearest land, Cape Maria Van Diemen, the northwest corner of New Zealand. In late afternoon the wind decreased to a mere forty knots, but it blew directly from where we wanted to go.

Twenty-five thousand miles and two years earlier the sails had been the proud product of one of the world's great sailmakers. Now the sails were rags, seam after seam re-stitched by hand at sea. I did not know how long they would hold, but we could not remain where we were. To wait for good weather in the Tasman is often a futile pastime. I raised the storm jib and the heavily reefed main, and we began to crawl slowly north.

For a week we worked toward the land, balanced precariously on the very edge of survival. Each day one or more sails required repair; each day I bailed eight to ten hours. And always the wind persisted from directly ahead. Repeated immersion in salt water inside the cabin had done my radio receivers no good, but occasionally a faint signal came through. I tried to get weather forecasts but when I finally succeeded, wished I hadn't. Australian radio proclaimed another cyclone to be wandering about the Tasman after battering the Queensland coast, but neglected to say where. This was worse than no news at all, and caused me exaggerated concern at every minor fluctuation of the barometer.

Still we were afloat and slowly the x's on the chart marking our position neared the elusive peninsula before us, until in mid-afternoon on March 12, a bee settled into EGREGIOUS's cockpit to welcome us to New Zealand, while we were still thirty miles offshore. A few hours later I smelled land, and that night we passed North Cape and turned the corner to head south one hundred and eighty miles to Auckland. There was a sense that we were safe. But it was false. The wind turned with us. Still a headwind. Still no rest.

Land was never more of a mixed blessing than the morning of March 15. Obstacles littered the sea between us and Auckland, particularly the final thirty-five miles or so, where I counted references in the Sailing Directions to more than forty islands and rocks. We needed a break from the wind, but I expected none.

Not long after dawn, we nearly had the final disaster when the main ripped from leach to luff above the second reef, while we were less than two miles to windward of a stark uninhabited mile-long rock called the South Poor Knight's Island. The wind was blowing from the southeast, causing me to anguish about where such a wind was when we were in the Tasman and would have welcomed it. EGREGIOUS would not come about under the jib alone. To change course I had to gybe. But where her bow pointed made no difference. Without the mainsail, we were being rapidly driven onto the cliffs to leeward.

Ignoring water which soon rose above the cabin sole and splashed across my feet, I stitched the sail as quickly as possible, pausing to dart a glance at the ever-nearer cliffs only when I had to stop to re-thread the needle. Then I stitched faster. Still it took three hours before the sail could be reset.

Great waves were dashing spray against rocks only a few hundred yards away. I re-reeved the reef lines and carefully hoisted the main. The rip was in a particularly bad location, an area of strain at the leech. As soon as it was up, it ripped again. Instantly, before the tear could extend across the sail, which would have been fatal—there was no time for so extensive a repair again—I let the halyard run. Then I cut two very rough patches and stitched them on with giant strokes. A poor job, but my only hope.

In ten minutes I raised the sail for what I knew would be the last time. I thought that we had not come all this way to be wrecked here ninety miles from safety. Hold. Hold for just thirty minutes. Perhaps even just twenty minutes. And then I can do more. But hold!

Somehow it did.

After easing off that treacherous lee shore and applying two more patches to the main while it remained set, we spent the afternoon threading our way between islands that loomed through a low mist and seemed to bear no resemblance to descriptions in the Sailing Directions. By late afternoon I became certain of our position as unmistakable Little Barrier Island appeared off our port bow.

Sunset found us well down the Hauraki Gulf, the loom of Auckland's lights clearly visible to the southwest. With the darkness the wind lightened and backed, giving us an easy reach across sheltered water. A gentle sail at last. I should have known better and had I not been so exhausted I would have. That very tranquility was almost to wreck us.

All I had to do was remain awake one more night. After one hundred and fifty nights and twenty thousand miles, only one more night. But as EGREGIOUS softly sailed on, I became more and more tired. At about 2:00 a.m. a very bright navigation light was abeam, which I correctly concluded was TiriTiri. Beneath a full moon, visibility was good and I could see that, although there were some islands ahead of us, we would not come upon them for well over an hour. The night was a romantic dream. Water lapped musically at the hull. Fatigue overcame me. I could safely sleep for an hour, I told myself as I went below and lay on my berth still fully dressed. And I was right: I could have slept safely for one hour. But I slept for two.

I was dreaming. I cannot now recall the dream, but I do remember that I was in a very deep sleep one instant and the next some part of my mind brought me wide awake with complete knowledge of exactly what had happened. I leapt to the companionway and looming over us was a great shadow. The jib sheet, tied to the tiller for self-steering, tangled. Frantically I ripped it free and slowly, so slowly, EGREGIOUS's bow swung back into the wind, back the way we had come.

Later I learned that rock was one of a group called the Noises. Judging distances in unfamiliar waters at night is difficult, but the Noises are not very big. I was quite definitely looking up at the crest of that shadow. It was a long way above me. But our speed was only about three knots. Perhaps we would have bounced off.

At dawn I turned us back toward Auckland and we slowly limped past Rangitoto Island and into the harbor on a bright, warm day.

My first impression was how quiet it was for a commercial port on a working day. I was surprised at how many sailboats were swinging at moorings in various coves along the shore. I shouted at a man aboard a yacht powering by, asking where I should go to clear with Customs. My voice sounded strange to me. I could not recall the last time I had heard it. He directed me to wharves at the foot of office buildings in the center of the city.

In San Diego I routinely sailed the engineless EGREGIOUS in and out of her slip in a marina, but I had not tried to stop her for months. The space between the wharves was wide enough, but the wind was patchy. I sailed back and forth twice, looking the situation over. Several sailboats were rafted up to the wharves. I lowered what was left of the mainsail and sailed in under jib alone, made a U-turn back into the wind, and came gently alongside a big ketch.

It was a few minutes before 2:00 p.m. Some office workers on their way back to work after lunch watched me. I asked one of them to notify Customs of my arrival.

EGREGIOUS and I remained at King's Wharf for two more days, until we could be towed to Half Moon Bay Marina, which at that time was the only place in Auckland with a travel lift which could handle the boat. Not until the moment when the cutter was actually removed from the water and settled in her cradle, a stream of water flowing for a change from rather than into a deceptively innocent appearing three-pronged hairline crack, did I feel we were truly safe. Then I slept for fourteen hours.

PART II

1978 - 1983

CHIDIOCK
TICHBORNE

CHIDIOCK TICHBORNE was a stock British built Drascombe Lugger.

Drascombe Luggers are yawl-rigged open boats, that is they have no decks. They are 18 feet long, have a 6-foot beam, centerboards which draw 4 feet down and 10 inches up, and weigh less than nine hundred pounds.

Using the EGREGIOUS circumnavigation as a baseline, I sought an even greater challenge, qualitative rather than merely quantitative, with even greater reliance on myself than on the boat. Not at all incidentally I needed to do this in a boat that did not cost much. In 1978 CHIDIOCK TICHBORNE cost $5,000.

She was a wonderful little boat and proved to be essentially indestructible. Naturally she was wet, but she sailed well, making passages nearly as fast as conventional boats more than twice her size. I came to think of her as a small dog, energetic, vital, always eager, a terrier if not a terror of the seas.

With a centerboard and yawl rig, she was easily balanced. I was usually able to get her to self-steer by tying the jib sheet to the tiller offset by shock cords to leeward, a method that had worked on EGREGIOUS when her windvane broke. I still navigated with a sextant. Actually several successive sextants, when my old one was lost during the swamping off Fiji.

I made the longest open boat voyage in history in CHIDIOCK TICHBORNE, more than twenty thousand miles with many stops west from California across the South Pacific to Australia up to Indonesia across the Indian Ocean and up the Red Sea, where I was briefly and falsely imprisoned as a spy. There were, in fact, two CHIDIOCKs. The first which I bought retail remained in Saudi Arabia. The following year the British builders kindly gave me a sistership and shipped it to Egypt, where I resumed the voyage, which ultimately ended in the Canary Islands.

During the four years from California to Saudi Arabia, I lost for the first time every single object I possessed in the world. I would lose everything again, but more quickly, in RESURGAM.

Chidiock Tichborne, the man, was executed for being a party to one of the plots to assassinate Elizabeth I. I seem to recall that he was caught because he had a bad leg that prevented him from running, while his co-conspirators escaped, but I will not swear to this. I had long admired the one poem for which he is remembered, written to his wife, and variously titled 'Tichborne's Elegy' or 'On the Eve of His Execution', and thought it proper to give an English-built boat an English-built name. The problem was in fitting a 19-foot name on an 18-foot boat.

---

1 9 7 8
June, took delivery of CHIDIOCK TICHBORNE from builder
November 12, sailed alone from San Diego for first attempted circumnavigation in open boat
December 16, arrived Nuku Hiva, Marquesas Islands

1 9 7 9
January 16, arrived in Tahiti
April—September, continued westward across South Pacific
September 11, arrived Suva, Fiji, where CHIDIOCK TICHBORNE was laid up for cyclone season

1 9 8 0
May 7, departed Suva, Fiji, for Port Moresby, Papua New Guinea
May 10, pitchpole and swamping, three hundred miles west of Fiji
May 10-24, adrift
May 24, reached Emae Island , in what was then the New Hebrides, now Vanuatu
October 9, repairs made, departed Port Vila for Australia
October 27, arrived Cairns, Australia

1 9 8 1
April—August, sailed north around Australia, to Indonesia and Singapore

1 9 8 2
sailed Singapore to Aden non-stop, then up Red Sea, arriving Port Sudan on March 12

May 29, left Port Sudan for Suez

June 4, put into Rabigh, Saudi Arabia to fit spare rudder; jailed as spy

June 15, compelled to depart Saudi Arabia by air; CHIDIOCK TICHBORNE remained behind

1 9 8 3

unable to obtain permission to return to Saudi Arabia, flew to England where Honnor Marine gave me sistership Drascombe Lugger, named CHIDIOCK TICHBORNE II, and shipped her to Egypt

May—June, flew to Egypt, launched CHIDIOCK TICHBORNE II at Suez, sailed down Red Sea to previous year's track in CHIDIOCK TICHBORNE I, then north to the Mediterranean, west to Malta

August, sailed CHIDIOCK TICHBORNE II from Malta to Vilamoura

October, sailed CHIDIOCK TICHBORNE II from Vilamoura, Portugal for Caribbean

November, stopped at Santa Cruz de la Palma, Canary Islands, to wait out headwinds; storm capsized CHIDIOCK TICHBORNE II on mooring in harbor; open boat voyage ended

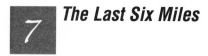

The Last Six Miles

As darkness fell on Friday, January 12, 1979, I hove to just east of Venus Point, six miles from Papeete, Tahiti. At 4:00 p.m. on Tuesday, January 16, after countless swampings and a final thirty-five hours continuously at the tiller, I sailed through Papeete Pass.

Until that final—or what I so mistakenly thought would be final—night before making port, the passage from Nuku Hiva in the Marquesas Islands had been uneventful. The entries in my log from January 2, when I raised anchor and sailed out of Taiohae Bay under blue skies, to January 8, when four hundred and twenty miles to the southwest I sighted Takaroa in the Tuamotu Archipelago, were almost identical: "Sunny. Hot. Slow." The wind blew steadily at seven knots; our speed hovered around three knots; our daily runs were a predictable sixty to seventy miles.

I sailed CHIDIOCK TICHBORNE not just to make good the best course to Tahiti, but also to take advantage of the shade from her sails, gybing at midday from a starboard broad reach to a port one. With the sun more than 80° above the horizon, there was nothing I could do about those scorching noon hours except cover my head with a wet towel, stretch out on the floorboards, and try to doze through the worst of the heat. The hats washed overboard between San Diego and Nuku Hiva—and irreplaceable in Nuku Hiva— were sorely missed. In fact, this inability to replace in Nuku Hiva so many of the things I had lost or damaged was one of the reasons I sailed so soon for Tahiti. The other, and more compelling, reason was that I wanted to talk to Suzanne, and in 1979, there were no telephone links from Nuku Hiva.

The first time I sailed to Tahiti I had sailed around the western end of the Tuamotus. This time, however, I was fully equipped with charts and planned, unless the weather deteriorated, to sail directly through—although I recalled meeting two sailors in the Society Islands who had lost their boats in the Tuamotus, and would meet, even in the age of electronic navigation, others who did so later.

My original plan was to sail toward the islands of Manihi and Ahe; but the wind kept me farther east. My morning sights on January 8, which indicated I should be near Takaroa, were verified when a tiny irregularity on the horizon satisfactorily became palm trees, around noon.

It was pleasant to have something to look at that afternoon as we sailed a few miles off palm-covered islets, first Takaroa, and then the neighboring atoll of Takapoto.

We were through the front door, fortunate to have made landfall under such fine conditions and to know by the proximity of land our precise position at sunset. But now we were sailing into a dangerous watery room. Ahead of us there were more reefs than there were gaps between them. The closest, Aratika, was fifty miles away and, as the wind increased and backed to the north, became a lee shore directly ahead of us.

Without the variable of unknown current, I would have worried much less. The problem was twofold: avoid running into anything that night, yet plan a course that would provide a landfall the following day. I did not want to spend two nights stumbling around in the darkness. I decided to continue south for about thirty miles, then gybe to the west.

For once the wind cooperated, and we had the best—in retrospect, the only good—sailing of the passage, making a steady four knots beneath a partially cloud-covered sky. I slept fitfully, peering into the darkness every thirty minutes or so, until 2:00 a.m., when I made the turn to the west.

Nothing went crunch for the rest of the night, and dawn brought one of the more noteworthy events in my years at sea: I caught my first fish. On previous and subsequent voyages I did not bother to carry fishing gear, but before I left San Diego this time a friend gave me some handlines as possible survival gear. On the passage to Nuku Hiva, I was kept sufficiently busy and did not use them; but on the second slow day out of Nuku Hiva, I set a couple of lures over the stern. I was surprised to find a twenty-pound tuna on one of those lines when I awoke. He was still alive, and I set him free. It seemed unjust to kill a fish that size for one meal. Not to mention too messy. I caught another, smaller fish two dawns later. And then, having proven I could, I stopped.

Until the advent of SatNav and later, GPS, I navigated on sun sights, common sense, and suspicion. Even with GPS the sailor would do well to be suspicious when charts of the South Pacific are covered with notes warning that all these islands may not be where they have been drawn, apparently at the whim of some junior clerk, and based, all too often, upon surveys circa 1879. So I was pleased when at 10:30 a.m. the palm fronds of Apataki appeared where I expected them to, off the port bow.

Apataki is shaped roughly like a rectangle and has two passes into the lagoon, one at the northwest corner and one at the southwest near the only village. For fourteen miles I sailed along an almost continuous pristine white-sand beach beyond which stood a green band of palms. It was my first sight of what was effectively a desert island, and the temptation to linger was strong. A thundercloud that made a brief appearance just as we were off the northwest pass, a non-functioning stove, and Suzanne, combined to keep me moving onward.

There were two more atolls to avoid that night, but with Apataki in sight at sunset, plotting a safe course was not difficult. By midnight we were well beyond the last hazard, with Tahiti one hundred and eighty miles of clear water ahead.

On Thursday I finally permitted myself to speculate about how many more nights at sea. With luck we would be in before Friday sunset, but an arrival Saturday morning seemed more likely, particularly when the wind continued to back, the sky grew cloudier, and the sea, rougher.

A single early morning sun sight on January 11 was to be the last of that passage. Finding Tahiti by dead reckoning from a distance of less than one hundred and eighty miles should not be difficult, but I did wish that the radio direction finder had not drowned, so I could home in on the beacon at Venus Point.

Conditions continued to deteriorate. By noon Friday we were sailing close-hauled with reefed sails on course 235° against eighteen knots of wind and four-foot waves, and taking a lot of water over the bow. Four-foot waves on CHIDIOCK were very different from four-foot waves on EGREGIOUS. It was unpleasant but not serious, so I kept CHIDIOCK to it, while I tried in vain to will more substance to various island-shaped clouds than they were able to sustain.

At last in mid-afternoon a firm silhouette became and remained distinct on the horizon. Tahiti was safely in view. As we sailed closer, I recognized Venus Point and hove to a few miles east at sunset.

It was the wrong decision made for the right reasons. Although I knew the pass fairly well, I have never liked to enter harbors at night. Obviously a storm was approaching, but that provided even more reason to wait until daylight. Visibility could be reduced to a boat length in seconds and the reef on the north coast become a lee shore. After all, I told myself, one more night at sea does not matter and you only have six miles to go. Sleep awhile, get an early start, and we'll be in Papeete in time to check for mail before the post office closes.

That the universe was once again not to adhere to my plans became evident at 11:00 p.m., when I was awakened by a flood. I had hove to by lowering the mainsail, trimming the mizzen flat, and backing the jib: standard procedure. But a gust came along powerful enough to heel CHIDIOCK over so far even under reduced sail that what should have been a drain on the starboard seat became instead an intake. When I located the source of the flow, I furled the jib and pumped CHIDIOCK more or less dry.

Venus Point Light still winked at us from the same relative bearing, and other lights upon the shore appeared unchanged. Then, in an instant, all the lights went out, heavy rain fell, and the little yawl began to go backwards very rapidly.

CHIDIOCK hove to well under mizzen alone, and we had an ocean of sea room to the east, so there was no immediate danger. As I expected the squall did not last long. But when it passed, Venus Point was obviously more distant, and the wind, although less strong than in the squall, held at more than twenty knots. Perhaps had I raised sail we could still have made it into Papeete, but I thought then—and still think—it best to wait until dawn. Surely we would make port some time Saturday, even if the post office had already closed. After all, we only had eight miles to go.

At 4:00 a.m., in pitch darkness, with no shore lights or stars visible, I struggled for half an hour to make myself a cup of coffee. The stove, jury-rigged with tape and waxed string in Nuku Hiva, proved equal to the challenge of preparing what I expected to be my last hot food before making port. In this, at least, I was correct.

I had drunk less than a third of the cup, however, when a wave swept over us. For some reason, I found it difficult to maintain aboard CHIDIOCK the stoic silence I managed on EGREGIOUS. In vivid images, I told the ocean what I thought of it, then I raised the jib, and we began pounding northwest toward where Tahiti—now an uncertain distance away in the darkness—must lie.

I had no fear of sailing blindly onto the reef. We would be lucky, I thought, to sight land again by 7:00 a.m., which, as it happened, was exactly when I did see land, or at least glimpse it, though clouds before another squall hit. That glimpse gave me the impression that we had fought back to the same position where we had first hove to. This raised my spirits, until the next break in the clouds revealed a long stretch of coast miles north of us. It was not Venus Point I had seen but another point far to the south, probably Point Tautira. Papeete was not six miles away, but twenty-eight, all of them to windward. For the first time I began to doubt that we would be safely at anchor that day. And then the storm began in earnest. Everything thus far had only been in the nature of a warm-up. I proceeded on a reluctant circumnavigation of Tahiti the hard way.

CHIDIOCK could not sail against the forty-five- to fifty-knot winds in the next squall, so I let her run off under jib and mizzen, thinking—hoping, anyway—that we might find some shelter around the end of the island.

It was one of the fastest rides I ever had aboard CHIDIOCK. The boat-speed indicator read to ten knots, and often the needle held there, not just when we were surfing down waves, but for sustained periods. CHIDIOCK made a couple of attempts to broach, but responded each time to the tiller before matters got seriously out of hand. Finally the 4,000-feet-high mountains at the south end of the island began to block the wind, the sky cleared somewhat, and we sailed into an area of wonderfully smooth water directly off the reef.

As was to occur frequently during the coming days, I found myself an indifferent spectator to scenes of great beauty. Green mountains; waterfalls—on Monday I was to count eleven waterfalls visible at once; misty, mysterious valleys. The picturesque held no charm for me. My only thoughts were of relief that CHIDIOCK had somehow once again held together, and of how to gather the energy to pump her out.

When patches of blue sky appeared, I began to hope that the worst was over. Around noon I ate the last handful of raisins. We had gone from fifty knots of wind to five, which lured me into raising the main. Under full canvas CHIDIOCK gurgled gently along, swinging wide to avoid the corner of the reef. I hardened up the sheets, and once again we headed northwest for Papeete, this time, however, up the western side of the island.

Until 4:00 p.m. we made good progress, but then with less than fifteen miles to go a sudden gust laid CHIDIOCK far over. Before I could release the sheets the little yawl was full of water.

By the time I had finished bailing, the wind was shrieking at more than fifty knots and the waves were steep and breaking. I knew there was nothing to do but let CHIDIOCK ride them hove to under mizzen, although I did set out a sea anchor to try to reduce our drift. The sea anchor was not effective, CHIDIOCK was blown backwards so fast that her stern developed a bow wave.

With nightfall coming on—a night I had once been certain would find me clean and dry and relaxed in Papeete Harbor—I found myself wet and cold and depressed. I was not hungry, somewhat surprisingly, for I had eaten nothing all day except the few sips of coffee and the handful of raisins. I turned my face once again into the wind just to make certain that it was truly hopeless, before reluctantly wrapping myself in the tarp and lying down. I wondered if CHIDIOCK would survive the night and, if she did, how far away the dawn would find us.

When a sailor is tired enough, he can sleep anywhere, even in an 18-foot open boat in a full gale. I fell into a fitful slumber until midnight. The wind continued to shriek but the blinding rain had stopped by then and most of the eight-foot waves hissed harmlessly beneath us, although CHIDIOCK persisted in trying alternately to stand on her bow and on her stern. The clothes beneath my foul-weather gear were soaking wet, and I resolved to try to change them, although this meant a prolonged struggle. Somehow, by a minor miracle, I managed. With momentarily dry clothes on, I found myself hungry and ate a can of chicken before again managing to sleep.

Sunday was a replay of Saturday. We fought our way to the northwest until Tahiti again became visible; then a squall hit—I was becoming very adept at heaving to—and we were blown helplessly backwards in the general direction of the Cook Islands, some six hundred miles away. More than once I thought that I might find it faster to sail there than the twenty or thirty miles to windward to Papeete.

Late Sunday afternoon saw another partial clearing and CHID-IOCK able to make distance to the north. When the island once again came in view, I was elated to see what I thought was the point of land on which the airport is located. Another silhouette through the clouds, I concluded, was Moorea. We had not been blown as far off as I had feared. And once again Papeete was less than ten miles away—though now ten miles to the northeast rather than ten miles northwest, as it had been forty-eight hours earlier. And once again I permitted myself to hope we would be in that night.

But as we sailed closer, the compass bearings to various points were wrong, and the Korean fishing boat wrecked on the reef and clearly visible in 1974 and 1976 did not appear. Neither of these omens bothered me particularly. The bearings would be wrong if I were misjudging our distance from the coast, and the fishing boat could have broken up in the past two years.

Something was definitely very odd, though, about the channel between Moorea and Tahiti. The islands were continuing to over-lap, when from our perspective as we sailed closer they should be moving apart. The explanation appeared from the crest of a high wave. There was no opening between 'Moorea' and 'Tahiti'. They were connected by a low isthmus. For a moment my tired mind could not comprehend how this could be. Then I knew that what I was looking at was not Moorea and Tahiti but the two parts of Tahiti itself, and the point of land was not the airport but the isth-mus at Taravao. I had made the same mistake twice from different sides of the island in two days. Then the wind died completely, and for the rest of the night we were becalmed.

Every hour, as was my habit, good weather or bad, I awakened and glanced about. We were in close to land; the boom of surf on the reef a mile away was loud. At 1:00 a.m. I saw the lights of a ship offshore to the south of us. Having no lights lit myself, I watched until I was certain the ship would pass well outside of us, and then I closed my eyes. Twenty minutes later they opened to stare up at running lights. A native smiled down at me from the bridge of a tugboat a few yards away, and simultaneously CHIDIOCK bobbed violently in her wake.

My heart beat wildly: much, much too close. Then I thought: "A tug ?" I turned south and there was her tow, another tug, perhaps eighty feet long, bearing down on us. And because the lead boat had swung far in to come over to satisfy his curiosity, the tow was swinging even further. There was still no wind and no time to set sail anyway. Fortunately, in my premature preparations to make port I had unlashed one set of oars, which I quickly put to use.

Time is an uneven medium. Those few seconds seemed infinite. I row. CHIDIOCK slowly gathers way. The sinister shape of the towed tug looms ever closer, swings ever more toward us. I row. The cable between the ships jerks taut, droops into the ocean, jerks taut again. I can see individual drops of water being flung aside. I row. Then she is upon us. Even at that last moment I expect to be hit. Silently the tow swings past, only inches away. I examine her rivet by rivet. And then she is gone.

The tugs have disappeared around the point long before my breathing returns to normal.

At 5:00 a.m. a breeze blew out from the land and, munching a handful of nuts—practically my only food the last two days—I settled myself at the helm for 'the duration'. Barring another flat calm, I had decided to stay at it until we got in.

I have seldom made such a decision. The last time before this was in 100-plus knot winds south of Australia in EGREGIOUS. The next would be in the Straits of Gibraltar years later. Now, off Tahiti, I was already very tired and thought I should make a final effort before the storm ground me down further. The proximity of land was itself a danger. My food supply was low—the swamping on Saturday had ruined all my rice. I was left with only a few rusty cans of chicken and tuna and soup that were edible without cooking, which was impossible. I was bothered by a swiftly spreading skin infection on my hands and legs. And finally I had simply had enough of being "tossed and driven on the deep blue sea," as an old sea chantey so quaintly puts it.

For the next thirty-five hours I remained at the helm—except when bailing—through countless squalls and swampings. After the first three or four, the cockpit was officially renamed 'Lake Chidiock', and a lifeguard was posted, who also took data for tide and current studies.

The wind did not reach the fifty-plus knot fury of Saturday night but regularly gusted above forty knots and regularly knocked CHIDIOCK down, even under jib and mizzen. Once when the jib sheet jammed, we experienced a new record high-water mark, one from which I feared we could not recover. Yet the little yawl came up and I bailed her out.

Slowly, very slowly, often at a rate of less than a mile an hour, we made progress to the north. By noon the point of Maraa was abeam. An hour later, after one of our knockdowns, a Papeete fishing boat powered over to offer us a tow. Although I very much wanted to accept, I could not bring myself to do so, and watched as they circled, waved, and sped off. My spirits fell a little with the knowledge that they would be in before the next squall.

I had no problem in staying awake that night: more rain fell on me than on Noah. Part of the time Moorea—the real Moorea—was in view abeam, and occasionally the lights of Papeete—the real Papeete—were visible to the east. But every time I tried to sail toward them, heavy wind and rain closed in and I had to tack back west.

Tuesday morning found the storm weakening, although it was to regain strength on Wednesday and last five more days. But, in the moderate interval, we managed at last to beat our way to and through Papeete Pass, having made good six miles in four days.

CHIDIOCK was easy to anchor, but I was so tired I botched my first attempt. For so long my only thought had been, "Get to Papeete," that when I finally did, I had nothing left. The rode did not run freely; before I could clear the snarl, my anchor had caught on the chain of a large ketch. The owner proved understanding, and I rested there for a while, until I managed to get CHIDIOCK temporarily settled. A few minutes later some fellow sailors rowed over and saved my life with a bowl of chili.

Adrift

Each night I lost something. On the night before I was to leave Suva, Fiji, I misplaced my copy of *War and Remembrance* with three hundred pages unread and had to buy another copy to learn how World War II turned out. And once underway I lost two buckets, six gallons of fresh water, the moon, and then, in effect, CHIDIOCK TICHBORNE herself. It seemed almost as though fate and the sea were methodically reducing me to the minimum for survival.

I left the Royal Suva Yacht Club dock at 11:00 a.m. on Wednesday, May 7, 1980. The packing and plastic bagging and stowing had taken longer than usual, although CHIDIOCK TICHBORNE was carrying less than the load to which she had been accustomed the previous year. What was routine when I was moving on every month or so now had to be thought through and planned; but by 10:30 everything was in place. I had cleared Customs the preceding day, and Immigration had come by that morning—both special courtesies so that CHIDIOCK would not have to go alongside the main Customs dock, which was scaled for ships rather than 18-foot open boats. I still had a dollar of Fijian small change, so I walked up the dock to the yacht club bar and ordered a pitcher of Chapman's, a soft-drink mixture of ginger ale and bitters. Although I had worked up a thirst in the morning sun, a full pitcher was too much and no one was around to share it with. Quickly I downed three or four glasses, but I was eager to be off and left the half-full pitcher on the table. Within a week I would be dreaming of it: bubbles rising through amber liquid, ice cubes tinkling, beads of condensation running down the sides.

During her layover for the cyclone season, CHIDIOCK had become a wildlife refuge. Toads croaked from the moist darkness beneath her hull; a colony of ants built a nest in the centerboard well; birds found her gunwale a convenient perch; and a gecko took up residence in the cockpit. Surprisingly, but perhaps because of the gecko, there were no cockroaches aboard.

I did not see the gecko until I returned CHIDIOCK to the water and was living aboard her at the yacht club anchorage. Then, sometimes in the evening when I was reading by the kerosene lamp, I would catch a glimpse of the little lizard scurrying across the periphery of light. For his own good I tried to catch him and return him to the safety of the shore. Even the best of passages aboard CHIDIOCK is not something to be wished on a gecko; but he easily evaded pursuit. So as CHIDIOCK TICHBORNE sailed out Suva Pass into the predicted rough southeast swells, I half expected to see a poor seasick lizard, greener than usual, climb groggily onto the seat, stand on tiptoe, and peer longingly back at the receding hills. It did not happen. In fact I did not see him again. I like to think that he got off before it was too late.

I had cleared for Port Moresby two thousand miles west and north, where I hoped to obtain the necessary yacht permit from the Indonesian embassy so that I could continue quickly on to Bali. On the chart it was a straightforward passage, the only tactical decision being whether to make the move north before or after passing what were then the New Hebrides. First we had to get clear of the reefs immediately around Viti Levu.

Although I had twice sailed along that coast in other boats, I almost found myself embayed several times by long projections of the main reef reaching far offshore, particularly in the passage between Viti Levu and Beqa. The wind was steady at twenty knots, but the waves were disproportionately high. The forecast was for up to twenty-five-knot winds and twelve-foot waves off the west end of the island. Conditions approached that near Suva, with cresting ten-foot waves in the narrowest part of the passage, through which I had to steer by hand.

By late afternoon we were past Beqa. I was able to get CHIDIOCK to balance long enough so that I could eat a can of tuna. A ketch appeared from the west, tacked twice, and headed toward me. As she came close I saw that despite being fifty feet long, she was working hard going to windward. She crossed ahead of us and fell off to reach alongside on a parallel course. Part of her rub rail had worked loose. A jib dangled from the bow. The three crew on deck were haggard.

"What island is that?" a bearded man in foulweather gear called. He was pointing south.

"Beqa," I shouted above the wind.

He relayed the word to someone in the cabin. Then, "Can you spell it?"

I did, adding that there is an alternate spelling beginning with an M on some charts.

The larger boat was moving past CHIDIOCK and the man yelled to the cockpit crew to let the jib slat. "And where is Suva?"

This was more than I expected. I pointed back to the northeast. "About thirty miles. But there is a good anchorage on this side of the small island to the west of Beqa."

"Our engine is broken," the man cried, as the big ketch surged beyond shouting distance.

They turned into the wind and hardened up on the sheets. When they were again close enough, I yelled a warning about the reefs. They waved and disappeared into the gloomy dusk. I sailed around the world before I returned to Fiji and learned that they lost their boat that night on the reef.

A few hours later the light marking the island of Vatu Leile, about twenty miles south, and the last obstacle before we had open ocean to the New Hebrides, appeared off the port bow. The wind and waves had increased. CHIDIOCK was sliding down waterfalls, constantly on the verge of either broaching or gybing. Despite having the jib sheeted to the tiller and balanced by four shock cords, I had to keep my hand on the tiller. But sometimes we still gybed when, despite my putting the helm hard over, the stern was carried through the wind by a wave. The force of the wind was so great when this happened that I had to use both arms to bring the tiny yawl back on course. Some return to the sea, I thought. Or is this normal and I've forgotten? Several waves swept CHIDIOCK, but I did not discover the consequences until morning.

By midnight the light on Vatu Leile was well astern. I knew that we had made more than sixty miles since noon. I was tired, and there was no reason to exhaust myself by steering through the night, so I hove to for a few hours' sleep.

At dawn the wind and waves were still high, the waves higher than those in the fifty-knot storm we had been in around Tahiti, perhaps as high as fifteen feet, though the wind was only thirty knots. I reached for the small water jug I kept lashed to the mizzen mast for daily use. It was not there. More irritated than alarmed, I crawled back to see if it had fallen beneath the inflatable dinghy lashed to the stern locker. But it was gone. The passage to Port Moresby should take three or four weeks and I had debated carrying three or four of the collapsible five-gallon water containers, in addition to the small, one-gallon jug. Because CHIDIOCK was stern-heavy when loaded, I did fill a fourth container and lashed it to the bow cleat. Now I saw that it too was gone, leaving behind only its nicely secured handle. Overnight, twenty-one gallons of water had been reduced to fifteen—more than ample, but distressing.

After eating a granola bar and drinking a cup of cold coffee, I tried to get underway again. A wave caught CHIDIOCK just as I was turning her and threw us sideways a couple of boat lengths. Once we completed the turn and the wind steadied on the port quarter, I was able to get her to steer herself as we fled westward at six knots.

Steadily throughout a day of fast if wet sailing, we made our way through the worst of the band of rough water off Viti Levu. The odd wave continued to break, but now the waves were in the six- to ten-foot range, and the wind had dropped to twenty knots. That second night I was able to let CHIDIOCK continue to sail, although I slept very lightly, a part of my mind alert to an accidental gybe, which threatened every half hour or so. Usually I awakened in time, but twice I was too late and we were hammered. I knew I was pushing her too hard, that it would be safer to heave to, but I also knew that every mile was carrying us out of the rough seas.

The next morning I found that the two buckets, one inside the other, that I used as the head, had washed away, leaving—as had the water container—their handles neatly lashed behind. I had one bucket left, but I began to wonder what would be next.

All that day, Friday, conditions improved, although I still could not get the stove to remain lit or manage a sun sight. That night we lost nothing except the last sliver of the waning moon, hidden by clouds.

Saturday, wind and waves dropped further to about eighteen knots and four to six feet respectively. Saturday night I fell asleep at 8:00 p.m. in the belief that I would have my first real rest since leaving Suva.

Just before 10:30—when I looked at my watch a few minutes later it was 10:33—CHIDIOCK slid down a wave and pitchpoled. It is difficult to separate what I concluded upon reflection must have happened from my sensations at the time. One moment I was sleeping wrapped in the tarp on the port side of the cockpit, and the next I was flying through the air, catapulted like a pebble, as the stern came up. Dimly I recalled a clank, seemingly metal to metal, and then the stern rising behind me. I was afraid it would come down on me, that I would be impaled by the mizzen mast. Then I was in the water. I struggled free from the tarp, choked as a wave passed, and swam the five yards back to CHIDIOCK. I believe that given time she would have righted herself, but when I reached her, she was on her starboard side, her masts 30° below the water. Worse than last time, I thought as I swam around the bow. When I put my weight on the centerboard, she staggered upright.

I flopped over the side, which was not difficult. The gunwale was level with the sea. Much worse than last time. I fumbled beneath the water for my eyeglasses and found them still wedged in place by the bilge pump.

CHIDIOCK TICHBORNE felt as though she were sinking. Except for a few inches at the bow, she was completely below the water. With each wave, she dropped from beneath me and I thought that she was gone. But each time she came back. The sails cracked in the wind. The pitchpole had been explosive and the jib and main were ripped along the leech tapes. The mizzen mast support bracket was broken, and the mast and sail floated astern. I pulled them back inside the hull, though I do not know why I bothered. Inside, outside, there was no difference.

Food bags, clothing bags, the bag with navigation tables, all were secured to a long line tied to the mainmast, and all were bobbing around the surface. An oar floated away, as did a bag I recognized as containing books. It was still within arm's reach and I could have saved it—later I regretted that I didn't—but it did not seem important at the time.

A mess of lines writhed like snakes. I felt beneath the sea for the jib-furling line. We were lying beam on to the waves, the sails trimmed for a broad reach, and by the time I furled the jib and found and released the main halyard, both sails were in shreds.

Another oar floated into the darkness. The cloud cover was complete, broken by not even a single star. Beneath the black sea CHIDIOCK was unfamiliar. I could only reach into the depths blindly, catch an object, and lift it to my face for identification. So far surprisingly little seemed to have been lost. But I could not find the last bucket. Only a plastic bowl was left to use to bail.

Gradually I gained confidence that CHIDIOCK TICHBORNE was not going to sink. She was, as a former friend liked to say, an object for going out, rather than an object for going down. And had I been able to clear the water from her within those first hours, we could have resumed sailing not much the worse for wear.

I had contemplated such a swamping and made preparations, but the reality was more chaotic than I expected. The unsolvable problem was the centerboard slot. I had cut two pieces of wood to screw into place to block this slot, but in more than six thousand miles, even in an earlier capsize in which I was thrown from the boat on the passage from San Diego to the Marquesas, I had not needed them. When last seen they were in the forward starboard bin with the spare anchor rode, now hopelessly twisted with the mainsheet, bags, oars, and tattered pieces of sail. I waded forward gingerly—with each movement CHIDIOCK dropped away like an express elevator—but I could not find them. Presumably they had already floated away. With a sense of futility I gave up the search, returned aft, and sat down in waist-deep water. I took my little bowl and began to bail. I did not expect it would do any good, but I did not have anything else to do that night.

CHIDIOCK almost seemed to help, to try and ride higher, though probably it was only that the waves decreased a bit without my noticing, and gradually I made some progress. The gunwales were now sometimes an inch or two above the sea. I stopped bailing and stuffed some pieces from my foam sleeping pad around the centerboard, but turbulence carried them away.

After another hour of bailing, I permitted myself some hope. We had several inches of freeboard, the seats were usually clear, and the water was mostly confined to the cockpit well. Only four more inches and I would reach the top of the centerboard trunk. But it did not happen. For two more hours I struggled without gaining even a fraction of an inch. The Pacific Ocean and I had reached equilibrium. Whenever I thought I might be gaining, CHIDIOCK would heel a few degrees and take on more water.

At 3:30 a.m. my back cramped. I was very tired. Perhaps the answer was to wait until dawn, jettison everything not absolutely essential that had not already jettisoned itself, and try again.

CHIDIOCK was too awash to permit any useful rest, so I inflated the dinghy, pumping a foot pump by hand. When the dinghy could support me, I secured it to CHIDIOCK with two lines and fell inside. Soaked to the skin beneath my foulwater gear and no longer warmed by exertion, I lay shivering through the remainder of the night.

By 6:00 a.m. I was back aboard CHIDIOCK. She seemed deeper in the water than when I left her. I transferred the food bag and the two remaining water containers to the dinghy. One container held about a gallon and a half of slightly brackish water; the other, a gallon. The third container had been punctured during the night. I also moved the navigation bag, the document bag, a Nikonos camera, two of the three compasses, the sextant, the solar still, the big tarp, and two bags of clothes. The clothes were not important, but I had already learned that even a small amount of water in the inflatable made rest difficult, and I wanted the bags to lie upon.

Almost everything else I threw away: the spare rudder; a box of screws and bolts; the typewriter; two new camp stoves; camera equipment, which I had trusted to an allegedly watertight aluminum case that wasn't; and the kerosene lamps. When I untied the main securing lines and opened the aft locker, other things I would have liked to keep, such as the medicine kit, a suit of brand-new sails, and an underwater flashlight, washed away.

Finally, one way or the other, CHIDIOCK TICHBORNE was stripped of all but her fifteen pound CQR anchor and rode, which I thought would be useful if we ever reached land.

Once again I settled in with my bowl and once again I made progress to the same level of four inches of water over the centerboard trunk. No matter how furiously I scooped, that, once again, was all.

Every hour my back cramped and I had to flop into the dinghy to rest. With such breaks I continued to bail through the day.

In late afternoon I accepted the inevitable and climbed into the dinghy, this time to stay. I sprawled on the clothes bags. Something hard dug into my leg. Too exhausted to sit up, I squirmed until it slipped to one side. I noticed that the sextant case had washed away, but I did not care. The navigation bag was beneath my head. I pictured the chart. Navigation had been by dead reckoning all the way from Suva. We were probably halfway between Fiji and the New Hebrides, 18° or 19° S, 172° or 173° E. Not very precise, but what did it matter? Three hundred miles from the nearest land.

The dinghy spun so that I could see CHIDIOCK TICHBORNE. Torn sails snapped. The mizzen mast floated off the stern again. I should do something, I thought, but I did not move. I just lay there, thinking how much had changed and how quickly, in the passing of a single wave.

At dawn and dusk I looked for land, even though no land could be near. And during the day I looked for ships, even though we were far from shipping lanes. I do not pretend that I would not have welcomed rescue, but I was forced to live up to my admonition to save myself, to rely on no one. For the present the wisest action was no action. Enforced passivity is one of the great facts of being adrift. Uncertainty about duration is another. At any moment a ship could appear; or I could drift for months, slowly dying.

On this morning, Tuesday, May 20, the tenth day of living in the nine-foot inflatable, there were not even any good imitation cloud islands in sight. For more than an hour I sat on the side of the dinghy, more comfortable than when I was lying on the now saturated and rock-hard clothes bags in the bottom, which still was better than lying directly in the permanent pool of water beneath them. I had nothing new to look at, nothing new to think, nothing to read. The sun rose steadily; waves slopped over CHIDIOCK one hundred feet to windward; the wind blew at fifteen knots from the east-southeast; we continued to drift west-northwest at about one knot. Everything was as it had been the day before, and the day before that. Ironically, good weather settled in two days after the swamping, and we were missing fine sailing. I knew that if this wind carried all the way to Port Moresby, CHIDIOCK would have made her fastest passage ever.

I had had more than ample time to consider what we had struck and was reasonably certain that it was inanimate rather than animate. Great flukes towering over me would be a good but untrue story. No, it had been a log or a tree or, as I was inclined to believe, a container washed from a ship. CHIDIOCK's hull was unmarked, but with a draft of only ten inches that was to be expected. Only the centerboard had hit, and it had not sustained serious damage.

I glanced at my watch. 9:07. I could not wait any longer. Time for the big event of the day.

Sitting down on the yellow plastic clothes bags, I studied the waves. They were only three feet high and rarely coming aboard, but I was acutely aware that whenever I opened the three layers of plastic bags protecting the ship's stores, I was risking a month of life. Quickly I grabbed a handful of cabin crackers and the jar of raspberry jam, the joy of my existence.

Long ago the sea imposed on me the habit of eating fast. Aboard CHIDIOCK it was a matter of getting the food in my mouth before a wave ruined it. But being adrift effected a cure. I chewed each crumb slowly, completely, and those big enough to dip into the jam, even more slowly and more completely. I loved that jam so much that I could not bring myself to ration it. When it was gone, it was gone—probably in ten more days.

The last cracker crumbs eaten, I could not resist one last finger full of jam. I licked my finger clean before reluctantly returning the jar to the food bag. I waited a few more minutes before lifting the water container for my two morning sips. Sips, not mouthfuls, though occasionally the dinghy jostled when the container was to my lips and I swallowed more than intended. I was angry when this happened. I did not want to cheat. Jam was one thing, water quite another. As never before, I realized that the problem with the world's resources is distribution. A few too large sips meant a lost day of my carefully measured life. I might reach land in a few more days or weeks. A ship might appear at any minute. But if not, I intended to be alive for a long, if miserable, time. A minimum of sixty days, ninety or a hundred or more if I was able to catch rain.

On May 17, the first day I made any notes after the pitchpole, I wrote, "I will be alive in July. But June is going to be a long month." Two sips of water and two sips only. Each held in the mouth, savored, swished about, swallowed. They were gone. The long day loomed before me.

I tied the water container down and covered it with the corner of the tarp. There were three quarts of water left in that container, rainwater I caught by spreading the tarp between my feet and shoulders during a brief squall—a lovely few minutes.

We had not had much rain. Only that one squall was catchable, combining heavy rainfall with an absence of breaking waves that would spoil the water before I could scoop it up with the lid from an empty jar. In that squall I caught almost a full gallon of fresh water, in addition to drinking my fill. Another change: when sailing, I used to dodge squalls. Now I dreamed of them. I also dreamed of fountains and running-water faucets and iced tea and drinking from a hose on a hot summer's day, and worst of all, of the half-full pitcher of Chapman's I left at the Royal Suva Yacht Club. I found that incredible. How could I possibly have done such a thing? I vowed I would never leave a drink undrunk again. And then I realized that I might never have the opportunity again.

When I left Suva on May 7, I had twenty-one gallons of water aboard CHIDIOCK; when I settled into life aboard the inflatable on May 11, I had two gallons. Six gallons were lost the first night out, five gallons on the night of the pitchpole. At a generous estimate, I drank a gallon and a half between May 7 and 11. I could not help but wonder at such extravagance: had I ever really used half a gallon of water a day? That left six and a half gallons unaccounted for. I did not even bother to calculate how long I could live with that extra water: for practical purposes, forever.

Despite my meager diet, food was not a problem. I was not much bothered by hunger. I recalled a Kafka story, *The Hunger Artist*, in which the main character makes his living by performing fasts as a carnival sideshow. I too did not experience hunger after the first few days. But water was life, and I did not have eight and a half gallons on May 11, I had two and a half. With the rain, ten days later I still had two and a half gallons. But what had happened to the missing six gallons? Leakage? Evaporation? I do not know.

The solar still was a disappointment. As a test I once used such a still successfully, but now when it mattered, I could not get it to produce fresh water. And after I caught rain, I threw the still away.

The sun was warm enough for me to strip off my clothes and air my body. I was wearing the foulweather gear and the same shorts and shirt I had on at the time of the pitchpole. Digging into the clothes bags for a change was futile. Everything was wet and never really dried, but my skin felt better for being exposed to the sun.

My tan was very uneven. Hands, feet, and, I supposed, my face were dark brown; but most of the rest of my body was fish white—where it was not red with saltwater boils covering my forearms, buttocks, calves, and feet. A couple of spots on my buttocks, both elbows, my left wrist where my watch rubbed, and both feet, were ulcerated. Ointment helped, but I needed the miracle of being dry.

I looked over the side and tried to judge our speed: a knot? a half knot? The difference was significant: One hundred and sixty-eight miles a week or only eighty-four. I no longer needed to check the two compasses I had brought over to know our course: 280° True, just north of the sun's path, and unvarying for ten days. I feared any wind shift. I realized that in some ways we had been lucky—if unlucky to hit whatever we hit, then lucky to have done so three hundred miles east of the New Hebrides rather than west. And lucky to have steady wind blowing us in the right direction, even though such wind was to be expected in that part of the ocean. And most of all, lucky to have it happen this year when I had a good dinghy. I could have stayed alive aboard CHIDIOCK, but the effects of exposure would have been much worse.

A wave halfheartedly splashed aboard and soaked me, and I shifted to the other side of the dinghy to face the sun. From its height I knew it was nearly noon. I leaned over and opened the navigation bag, took a vitamin pill from the bottle, and closed the bag. Of all the things lost, I most regretted losing my sextant. It was a World War II Navy model manufactured by David White, two years younger than I was, and bought second hand for less than $100. It had taken me around the world, and I was fonder of it than any other possession. Everything else I needed to determine our exact position was in the navigation bag. In this, as in many other ways, the transition from yacht to dinghy was easier for me than it would have been for someone aboard a conventional craft. I was used to living in the open.

I put the pill in my mouth, lifted the water container for a single sip, and swallowed. Lunch.

Tomorrow there would be more. Cans were rusting and would

have to be used. The labels had come off the cans, but by shaking them I could usually guess the contents. Half a can of fruit cocktail for lunch, with the other half for dinner, which meant the only water I would use would be two sips in the morning.

My liquid supply was:

2 1/2 gallons of water

7 cans of fruit

3 cans of vegetables

10 small bottles of Coca-Cola

My liquid ration was less than one cup a day, six sips, or only five, depending on self-discipline at noon. I knew there was a possibility of kidney damage, but so far my kidneys functioned. I remembered Bombard's book about drinking sea water while drifting across the Atlantic, but I was not tempted to do so.

Each can of fruit or vegetables would provide liquid for a full day: ten days total. The water on hand would last at least forty days, and surely in these latitudes it would rain often. But I did not count rain in my calculations. Rain was a gift. The Coca-Cola, which I considered more secure in bottles than the water in plastic containers, was to be used last. Ten bottles for seventeen days, two days each for the first eight bottles. I had decided I would drink the last two bottles together. Once before I died, if only for a few minutes, I was not going to be thirsty.

My food supply consisted of:

5 cans ravioli

4 cans beans

1 can hot dogs

3 cans tuna

4 1/2 packages ship's crackers

3 boxes Muesli

1/2 jar jam

10 packages freeze-dried dinners

4 packets powdered milk

1 jar peanuts

1 can peanut brittle

1 bottle vitamin pills

Each can made two dinners, and the hot dogs would make three. I could stay alive a long time just on the crackers and Muesli.

The peanuts and peanut brittle would keep me going for weeks. And with caught rain, each freeze-dried dinner would last three days and each packet of milk, a week. Without rain, of course, the freeze-dried food was useless. I had eaten freeze-dried food without cooking, and I tried to eat some without water. It simply could not be swallowed. And probably it would have been counterproductive, drawing liquid from my body.

At times I wondered if I was being too hard on myself, particularly toward the end of the first week, when my body most strongly protested the new regimen. The odds were very good that I would come upon land within a month. And for a drift of only a month I would not have to ration much of anything. But if I did not come upon land, if the wind changed, or if I did see land but was unable to get ashore and had to continue to Australia, I was determined to last the course. I felt stronger that day than I had a few days earlier. In fact, I felt that for each of the past three days I had made some gain, however small; that I was reversing the inexorable slide toward death.

To escape the blinding heat Saturday afternoon, I had swum from the inflatable to CHIDIOCK. Already I had lost weight and strength, particularly in my legs. Back aboard CHIDIOCK, I made another search of her flooded interior and discovered treasure: two bottles of Coca-Cola, a knife, a tube of Desitin and one of sunscreen, a pair of shorts, a mismatched pair of thongs, a hammer, and a plate.

The knife had a bottle opener, and I immediately drank one of the Cokes. The other bottle still put me two days of life ahead, and the warm, sweet liquid did me a world of good. I pulled the inflatable to CHIDIOCK and transferred everything except the hammer and the plate.

Small fish, some electric blue, some almost transparent, swam inside CHIDIOCK. Someday, I thought, I may have to eat you.

The next day I again returned to CHIDIOCK, this time to try to bail her out after passing the tarp beneath the hull in an attempt to block the centerboard slot from below. The seas were calmer than at any time since she swamped, but it took me most of the morning to tie the tarp in place. I still had nothing suitable to use as a bailer. First I tried a plastic bag, which was worthless. I looked around and saw the plate. As a scoop it proved effective. I was able to move a considerable amount of water with it, but unfortunately not considerable enough.

Before untying the tarp and returning to the dinghy, I inserted the rudder and untangled the mainsheet and halyard. When I raised the torn sail, CHIDIOCK responded by gracefully rolling onto her side and sailing for the depths. Less gracefully, I leapt clear. She righted herself and I scrambled back aboard and was able to turn her downwind before she could repeat her new trick.

Grossly, very, very grossly, I was able to steer with great sweeping movements of the tiller, which was underwater. In an hour I might change her position by a hundred yards. But if I sighted land, even such limited control might make a difference. Inordinately pleased, I furled the sail and dropped the rudder back into the gaping aft locker before returning home.

From the beginning of the drift I held on to the hope that I could save CHIDIOCK TICHBORNE as well as myself, though I knew the odds against her were very long. That was one of the reasons I kept the boats tied together, even though the dinghy would drift faster by itself. I also thought that both boats together were more likely to be seen than either alone; and that, however unpleasant, the swamped CHIDIOCK TICHBORNE was someplace to go if the dinghy deflated. Now the odds against CHIDIOCK TICHBORNE seemed slightly reduced.

By mid-afternoon the sun was hot. I took the spare pair of shorts, dipped them in the sea, and put them over my head. I had already draped foulweather gear around my shoulders for shade. Unwashed, unshaven, uncombed, covered with more boils than Job, and with a pair of shorts as a turban, I was ready for the cover of *Gentlemen's Quarterly*.

I found myself speculating about other solo sailors who have been lost at sea: Slocum, Willis, Riving, Colas, Piver. I wondered if they died quickly or slowly. There had been times when I thought I was going to die at sea, but always death would have been quick. Now I was on the edge, not for a few minutes or a few hours, but weeks, months. Already my tongue was thick, my lips pasty. I wondered what it would feel like to be thirsty and know not that there was water that should not be drunk, but that there was no water. It was not death I feared, but the suffering along the way.

My initial reaction to being adrift was one of apathy laced with depression. I did not care about the voyage or the challenge or the sea. Sailing had brought more pain than pleasure. If I survived, I would go ashore and find a life with a little comfort—the old chimera: peace, rest, ease. Surely I had earned them.

But after a few days of this, I knew that if the sea did not kill me, and if it were possible, I would sail on. If CHIDIOCK were lost, I would try to replace her. I would not, however, sail indefinitely from shipwreck to shipwreck, disposing of open boats like used tissues. At a certain point, and I would know when, such a voyage would become absurd rather than honorable.

The terrible thing about the sea is that it is not alive. All man's pathetic adjectives are false. The sea is not cruel or angry or kind. The sea is insensate, a blind fragment of the universe, and kills us not in rage, but with indifference, as casual byproducts of its own unknowable harmony. Rage would be easier to understand and to accept.

Whenever I thought of death, and obviously I thought of it often, I also thought of Suzanne—not really an unflattering association. I was thirty-eight years old. No man in my family had lived to such an age for generations. I had accomplished some of what I wanted to with my life—not all, but more than most men. And for me dying at sea had long been accepted as an occupational hazard. Of all that the shore offers—the places I had not seen, the few friends with whom I would like to share some conversation and a bottle, the music, the books, the paintings—most of all, I would miss Suzanne. I had never loved her more than during these last days, when the contrast between the happiness we had shared and the bleak reality of the present was so great.

When I left Suva I had not realized that it was the very day on which four years earlier I left Auckland to sail for Tahiti. I had not known then whether I would ever see Suzanne again. Now, for quite different reasons, I also did not know if I would ever see her again. I was glad that I was not yet overdue, that she would have no reason to be worried.

Something on a nearby wave caught my eye, something brown and round now hidden in a trough. Then, there it was. It was going to drift past. Terribly excited, I dove over the side and started swimming.

73

When I had the coconut safely in the dinghy and held it to my ear, I heard the glorious sound of liquid. With the blade of my rigging knife, I cut away the husk, and with the fid, I punctured two of the eyes. Normally I am not fond of coconut, but the slightly sour liquid was ambrosia. I took two big swallows before draining the rest into a jar, almost two cups. And there was more moisture in the meat. But how to get to it? I recalled the hammer on CHIDIOCK and pulled us over. With three blows, the shell cracked apart: days and days of life.

Half an hour before sunset, I ate a dinner consisting of the last half of a can of tuna, washed down with coconut milk. Despite the can having been open for twenty-four hours, the fish did not smell bad. And I would have eaten it anyway.

In the last light, I searched for land. There was none. I wrapped myself in the tarp and tried to settle in for the long night of broken sleep. My thoughts were the same as they had been last night and the night before that. How many more long days and nights: four? forty? a hundred and four? And what was at the end: an island? a ship? death?

I drifted on.

The blackness was a cliff. I lost it for a moment behind the tattered remnant of mainsail. The time must be nearing 3:00 a.m. and I was sitting in chest-deep water, trying to steer the swamped CHIDIOCK TICHBORNE clear of the island, which, after promising life when I first spotted it the preceding morning, had become just another face of death.

Death at sea is protean. I had known it as water slopping about EGREGIOUS's bilge off Cape Horn; as the innocent-appearing crack at the trailing edge of the keel when I dove overboard in the horse latitudes; as disorientation when EGREGIOUS capsized in the Roaring Forties; as the sound of breaking waves when in the Southern Ocean I lay in my bunk and EGREGIOUS lay ahull, helplessly awaiting the wave that would finish her; as the incomparable force of wind south of Australia, ripping the surface from the sea, filling the air with water, making breathing all but impossible, as it drove EGREGIOUS beyond hull speed under bare poles; as the suddenly flooded cabin in the cyclone in the Tasman; as the slab side of the tug as it almost ran CHIDIOCK down off Tahiti. And now as this shadow, barely discernible against black sky and black sea.

Through rain-streaked glasses, I caught a glimpse of the ghostly line of surf at the base of the cliff, less than a quarter mile away. If we drifted much closer, I would have to abandon CHIDIOCK and take my chances in the inflatable. But I did not know if I could row the dinghy in such waves, now more than ten feet high and growing steeper as the long swell from the open ocean touched the rising seabed below. Perhaps I had already waited too long.

My body was filled with numbness and pain. I had been trying to steer CHIDIOCK for twelve of the past eighteen hours and for the last five hours continuously. The tiller and all of CHIDIOCK but the mast were below the water. There was an illusion of great speed caused by waves rolling over us. One of the waves crashed through the jib and tore it to ribbons. We were 'sailing' on the twenty or so square feet of chaffing patch on the mainsail. We were not truly sailing at all. I only hoped that by keeping the bow pointed generally in the direction of a broad reach, we might clear this first island.

From the waist down I had lost sensation, except for agony when I bumped the ulcers on my feet and ankles against the fiberglass floor. Moving the tiller through the exaggerated sculling movements necessary to control the swamped yawl took both hands, which had also lost feeling. I smiled inwardly when I recalled steering CHIDIOCK with a single finger. My back and neck were on fire. Always the fire smoldered and at intervals it flared into a spasm of white-hot pain. There was nothing to do at such moments but hang onto the tiller and wait for the pain to pass. Don't fail me, body. Don't fail before the sky begins to lighten.

A wave loomed high above me, the highest wave I had seen from CHIDIOCK, a wall of water as high as the yawl was long. Here we go, I thought. This one is going to break. CHIDIOCK started up the steep rise. The wave lifted me from her. I clung to the tiller, no longer steering, just hanging on until the tiller pointed straight up and I was floating at arm's length above the submerged hull. I was afraid not for CHIDIOCK but for the dinghy. Where was it? Downwind where it would be squashed beneath the yawl? I was nearly at the soaring crest. I had to let go of the tiller. CHIDIOCK turned beneath me, riding sideways up the curl. If only the oars weren't washed from the inflatable. Then I was through, sliding down the foaming back of the wave. Somehow it did not break, and an instant later CHIDIOCK and the dinghy came through unscathed.

I floated back aboard CHIDIOCK. Within a few yards the comber disappeared into the darkness, but I heard its roar as it slammed into the cliff.

We were not going to clear this end of the island. There was so much noise—sails, waves, surf, wind—that it was impossible to know whether my efforts were doing any good.

Under her scraps of sail I could not tack the yawl. I could not point any higher than a beam reach, which was not pointing at all, but merely CHIDIOCK's natural drifting position. Presumably I could gybe. I had not tried, for the wind was at right angles to the cliff and I was trying to clear the closer end. There seemed to be no advantage in gybing, and a clear disadvantage in that we would be in danger for a mile before reaching the far end of the island, rather than the two hundred yards to this end. But, as I hardly needed remind myself, we were not going to reach this end.

I pushed the tiller over, held it there, and waited. Another wave came and actually pushed CHIDIOCK in the opposite direction from the way I was trying to turn her. I kept the tiller over and kept waiting. With the next wave, the rudder gripped and her bow swung slowly off the wind. The motion, once begun, was assisted by a third wave; and with a fourth, the chaffing patch gybed and, from force of habit, I shifted to the other side of the cockpit.

The maneuver had cost distance. The cliff was now less than three hundred yards away and the waves were becoming steeper. I wondered if we had even a safe three hundred yards, if rocks or coral did not lie hidden beneath the breakers. CHIDIOCK was too low to provide an unobstructed view to the shore. I debated again whether I should abandon her and try to row free in the dinghy, since on this apparent course I was lengthening the distance to safety. Everything was 'apparent' because I simply did not know. Only after long minutes could I form any impression of true movement. Part of me screamed to get into the dinghy before it was too late, and part remained calm and said to wait a little longer until it was certain we could not clear the island this way either.

Without warning a wave broke. Because she was already beneath the sea, CHIDIOCK could not really capsize, but she rolled ponderously onto her side and I was washed away.

My legs were useless, circulation so impaired that commands to swim brought no response. They trailed like vestigial appendages on whatever form of life I was evolving into, as I fought first to keep myself afloat inside cumbersome foulweather gear and then to swim back to the yawl using only my arms.

CHIDIOCK TICHBORNE remained on her side. This view of her no longer seemed unusual. If anything, in the thirteen days since the pitchpole, I had come to have unlimited confidence in her. The sea could strip everything movable from her, toss her around like a toy, fill her with water; and she would patiently survive.

My legs persisted in their refusal to function, so I could not stand on the centerboard, but the weight of my upper body was enough to right the yawl. She actually had less water in her when I managed to get back aboard than before.

We had drifted closer to the island, but we also seemed to have drifted along. What was the direction? Days earlier I took the compass bracket to the dinghy in order to preserve it for my next boat. My exhausted mind worked slowly. With the coming of the first line squall last night—or rather, this night, but long ago, when I was resting in the dinghy—the wind had backed east, which meant that on a starboard reach we had been trying to clear the north end of the island, and now on port, the south end. I had thought that the current would likely follow the trend of the trade wind we had experienced for most of the two weeks adrift and tend north. But perhaps it divided. Perhaps there was a tidal variation. Perhaps all my struggling had been unnecessary. Perhaps if I had simply let us drift, we would have been saved by blind chance. For it was now obvious that we were being carried along the coast faster than we were being carried in. I could not yet be certain that we were being carried along fast enough, so I remained at the tiller, more or less holding the bow in the right direction. Even if this did no good, at least it did no harm.

Riding sideways up great curling waves just beyond a line of thundering surf, I fell asleep. My eyes closed and my head fell forward. Reflex snapped it back, which ignited the flames along my spine. Each spasm had been worse than the one before, and this was a summation. I wondered if it would ever end. Could so much pain come from a muscle spasm?

Whatever the cause, the pain served to keep me awake until we sailed, drifted, and were carried safely past the island, and I was able to collapse into the dinghy and rest.

Dawn was delayed by a squall. When it passed I saw that we were drifting down a great corridor of sea, bounded on the north by a line of four islands, and to the south by a large island in the far distance and several closer rocks, one of which was so white with guano that I mistook it for a sail. Six or seven miles directly ahead of us lay two more islands: one, a small, sheer peak jutting from the sea; the other, five miles long and with three 2,000-foot peaks, about which the squall line lingered. In the pallid light all the land was gray and showed no sign of habitation.

I pushed myself up and ate a breakfast of half a dozen crackers, raspberry jam, a can of pears, and a handful of peanuts, washed down with unlimited water. At the first sight of land rationing ended. The need for energy far outweighed the possibility that I might not be able to get ashore and have to drift on. I even drank two of the precious bottles of Coca-Cola.

When I completed this feast, I opened the navigation bag and studied the chart. There were only two groups of small islands, such as those surrounding us, shown in the New Hebrides. One was too far north, so we must be among the other group, just fifty miles north of Port Vila, the capital.

I found some small satisfaction in having my dead reckoning proven correct. I had predicted landfall in two weeks from the pitchpole, and here we were on Saturday, May 24, two weeks later to the day. My self-satisfaction was short-lived when I recalled the past night. I still had to reach shore alive.

I stared back at the islands behind me. With the coming of day, I was not certain which cliff had almost destroyed us. I turned to the island ahead. Rain was falling on the peaks. People must live there, I told myself.

Throughout the morning, waves marched forward regally and carried Chidiock Tichborne with them. I felt as though we were being escorted along a marble corridor in a great palace. The waves had not diminished, but now in deeper water, they were no longer breaking. The motion was stately; the mood, solemn, as I lay resting in the inflatable and watched the nameless land come nearer.

The size of the waves worried me, as did the nature of the shore. I knew little about the New Hebrides, except that it was at that time under joint British and French rule and was soon to gain independence and be renamed Vanuatu.

Of a few things I was certain: beyond the island ahead of me lay only the open ocean for fourteen hundred miles to Australia; landing would be safer on the leeward side of the island; I must be on land before night; I dreaded the physical pain of returning to CHIDIOCK. At 11:00 a.m. I did so anyway.

The ocean felt cold as I settled beside the tiller, perhaps because I was running a fever caused by the infection in my feet. With movement, circulation and sensation were restored. A necessity, I supposed, but a mixed blessing. Who would expect that the feet are the part of the body to suffer most in sailing an open boat? The familiar needle-and-pin pains shot through them. They were swollen with edema. And the ulcers, particularly on both ankles, where the rotten skin was easily bumped, were filled with pus. The first moment of reimmersion was almost unbearable, but then my feet and legs went numb and I forgot them.

As I tried to sail CHIDIOCK, the sun broke through the clouds and turned the small island bright green. For another hour the larger island remained shrouded, but then the sky cleared and it too turned emerald. And I saw a house. I could not take my eyes from it, the first outpost of man, which during the days adrift I had thought I might never see again. It was just a small house in a clearing on the side of the northernmost peak, and yet proof that someone actually did live on the island; and where they could live, I could live. A while later, a column of smoke rose from farther up the mountainside, where someone was clearing brush.

By then, though, conditions had changed. Once again, no matter how I tried to sail, CHIDIOCK was carried sideways by the current. If in the night the current had saved us, now the scales balanced, for we were being carried too far south, away from the land, which now meant life, not death.

When there were only three hours of daylight remaining, I knew that I could not get CHIDIOCK ashore before dark, if ever. Sadly I returned to the inflatable, cast off, and began to row. The gap between the boats widened. The dinghy rowed well as I quartered wind and wave. I was still too far off to determine anything of the shore, except that midway along the island mist filled the air as though from heavy surf. There was no question of rowing around to the leeward side. I had neither the time nor the strength, though I was buoyed by the certainty that an end would come before sunset.

As I rowed I gazed back at CHIDIOCK TICHBORNE. Perhaps her loss had been inevitable since the pitchpole. If I had been rescued by a ship, she would probably have had to be abandoned. And even if I had managed to maneuver her to land, if there were a reef, I would have had to let her go. But we had been through so much: seven thousand miles since San Diego. And at this very moment she was still sound. Despite everything, with a few replacements and a few repairs, she could continue the voyage. From only a short distance away, she was mostly hidden in the troughs, and I realized how unlikely had been the possibility of ever being spotted by a ship. Already she seemed well to the south on a course that would carry her outside the offshore peak. I waited for one last glimpse of her. There she was on a crest, torn sails fluttering, awash, valiant. I engraved this image in my mind and then deliberately turned away.

For an hour I rowed hard, managing to get across wind and current. Then I rested and drank a Coke as we drifted closer. Individual palm trees became distinguishable, and a second house on the hillside not far from the first, but no other signs of man: no fishing boats, no village that might mark a pass or a landing.

The waves started to build before I saw the beach and the reef. I was almost directly below the house, which stood perhaps a quarter mile back from the shore and a few hundred feet up the mountainside. The beach ran from the northern point, was obscured by brush, then appeared again for two hundred yards of pure white sand, before being lost in a jumble of rock. For a quarter mile out from the beach lay the smooth turquoise waters of a lagoon. Life. And between me and the lagoon lay the reef.

When I was close to the surf line, I began rowing along the shore, searching for a pass. There was none. Soon we were around the rocks, and the shore and reef fell away to the west. I could see an unbroken line of surf, between three and five breakers deep, increasing in violence in the distance.

I turned and tried to row back; but the dinghy was caught in the sweep of the seas. Suddenly the ocean changed color and I saw coral reaching toward me. Any place was as good as any other. The coral would slice me up, but if I could protect my head, I should survive. I turned in.

At first I went slowly, trying to get a feel for the rhythm of the waves. I backed water as the dinghy trembled on a crest that almost broke beneath us; then I rowed as hard as I could. The next wave rose. Still rowing I noted the lovely translucent blue of the water as it climbed to the sky. I even had time to think that this might be the last thing I ever noticed. The wave toppled and threw us out, up, and forward. The dinghy's bow was dropping, and I dove toward the stern in an attempt to balance it. Everything was roiling water. It passed and I came up for a breath, surprised to find myself still inside the dinghy, the oars still gripped in my hands. Another wave was coming and I resumed rowing.

The second wave was worse than the first. My sense of direction was lost. I fell backwards as the dinghy stood on its head while the wave swept us along. I forgot my intention to protect my head with my arms, and rose once again with oars in hand, rowing.

The third wave was smaller than the first two and less dangerous. I was able to keep my head above water, though neck deep in foam. Then it too passed and instinctively I was again rowing for my life. The moment when I realized that there was no need, that we were through, that we had made it without even a scratch, came abruptly. The wild ride over the reef, the days of doubt adrift, the solitary struggle, and now I was going to live. I really was going to live.

Once again I found myself chest deep in a swamped ship. Kneeling in the bottom of the dinghy, I rowed slowly across the lagoon. I was amazed that we had not capsized in the surf and that the oars had stayed in place. I owed much to that dinghy. If only I could have saved CHIDIOCK TICHBORNE.

A speck of color caught my eye. Several huts stood among the palm trees at the point; from one of them hung a line of drying clothes. Those pink and blue and white bits of cloth were symbols of normalcy that filled me with comfort.

I drifted the last few yards. Sand grated beneath the dinghy. I stepped ashore, my dead legs collapsed, and I fell. I lay there laughing.

The voyage had shattered like a vase, and the pieces were scattered around the world. As I limped along Cook's Beach on New Zealand's Coromandel Peninsula, I wondered if I would ever be able to put it back together again. I was no longer free to sail on. I was dependent on boat builders, business men, editors, publishers, shipping agents, dock workers, crewmen on freighters, on copra boats, customs officials, tribal chiefs, and revolutionaries. Adrift, life had been simple. Ashore it quickly became more complicated. As I told the official at the British Residency at Port Vila who expressed surprise that I managed to save my passport and traveler's checks, "I did not know if I would survive. But I knew that if I did, I would need little pieces of paper."

I had been ashore for two weeks now, the same length of time I was adrift, but vastly different. My feet and body were almost healed, my spirit less so. Perhaps as was only natural, when survival became certain, my will lapsed. And it was both fortunate and unfortunate that Suzanne and I were lent the use of a beach house.

Fortunate because Cook's Beach is a beautiful spot on the shore of Mercury Bay—Captain Cook stopped to take a transit of Mercury there, as he earlier did of Venus at what became Venus Point in Tahiti—with scenery and climate similar to Northern California, but, except during the summer Christmas vacation, with considerably fewer people. In June we almost never saw another soul when we collected driftwood for the fireplace, and seldom more than a few cars during the two mile walk to the nearest store. It was a fine, quiet place for me to recuperate and write and think.

But unfortunate because in my weakened condition I liked the place so much I wanted to stay. I found myself studying the smooth waters of Mercury Bay and thinking what a perfect place it was for a boat like CHIDIOCK TICHBORNE. There were coves and rocks and islands to explore for years, a home ashore, the comfort of Suzanne, and, undeniably, the avoidance of more pain. I had struggled against the sea for most of the past six years, and I was tired.

Bernard Moitessier said to me when we met in Moorea, "Ah, but you are young and strong." I was thirty-seven at the time. A little more than a year later, I felt old. When I attempted on my first circumnavigation to reach Cape Horn, I told myself that nothing else would ever matter so much in my life, and so I made the commitment absolute. Now, did this voyage too have to become a matter of victory or death? Was it that important to me? Would any lesser commitment enable me to continue? Was it worthwhile, or was I nothing more than a casual amusement, a sideshow freak like Kafka's hunger artist? Would I come this close to dying three times every seven thousand miles? And when would I have done enough? I held a world record for my first voyage and with CHID-IOCK TICHBORNE I had already sailed farther than any other man alone in an open boat. To paraphrase the great baseball pitcher Satchel Page, I looked back and didn't see anyone gaining on me.

As I continued along Cook's Beach, my mind turned from these unprofitable thoughts to that other, warmer beach a thousand miles north, and to my first moments ashore.

By the time I unloaded the dinghy, the sun had gone behind the mountain and the air was cooler. This was the tropics, so the temperature was still in the eighties. But because of fever, I was cold.

Looking for a change of clothes, I opened the bags and spread their contents on the sand. In addition to moldy clothing, navigation tables, documents, and food, I found that I had also shared the dinghy with such essentials as a road map of Tahiti and a hot-water bottle.

Apparently no one had seen me come over the reef, and I did not feel like walking the short distance to the village that night, meeting people, talking, explaining. I wanted a last night alone. It was enough to know that the village was there. I could wait until morning to rejoin the human race.

When I started to shiver, I wrapped myself in my old friend the tarp, variously a tent, roof, blanket, rain catcher, centerboard plug, and now ground cloth. I fell immediately asleep.

Dimly, through fathoms of fatigue, the murmur of the wind in the trees sounded like Elvis Presley; but even while sleeping this seemed odd, so odd that I knew something must be wrong. I sat bolt upright and threw off the tarp, causing thirty or so Melanesians, who thought a corpse was coming to life, to scream, shriek, gasp, run, and pray. One of them did indeed hold a portable cassette player from which came Elvis's voice.

"So, you are alive, then," said a tall man about thirty years old, one of the few onlookers who remained composed. He had a British accent.

"Yes. And very glad to be. I hit something with my sailboat and drifted for two weeks in that." I pointed at the dinghy. "Where am I?"

"On Emae Island."

"Can you show me on a chart?"

"I should think so." When I handed him the chart, he pointed to a small island about forty miles north of Port Vila, which was where I thought I was. Then it was the man's turn to ask questions.

"How did you come ashore? You did not come over the reef?"

"I couldn't find a pass."

"No. There is none on this side. You must have injured yourself."

"I was lucky. My feet are bad, but that was from before."

They all looked down at my puffy feet and gave a chorus of 'Oh's'.

"We must get you up to the chief's house. Can you walk just as far as the trees? I will send someone for the truck."

"Slowly."

"Of course. Take your time."

He said something in another language and everyone smiled. Several children ran off along the beach toward the village, while many others picked up pieces of my gear, and we made our way across the beach and through a line of brush to a trail cut through the jungle. I had not stood for almost three weeks, and my feet hurt too much, so I sat down on the damp ground and waited for the truck, which soon appeared bouncing along the ruts made by it and the one other vehicle on the island. Even though the young man who drove the truck did so carefully, I found the ride painful.

At the chief's house—as I expected it was the one I had seen from the sea—I was left in the care of Kalo Manaroto, his wife, Nellie, and their children. I never knew just how many children they had, for dozens were in and out of the place, and when I asked Kalo, he said, "Oh, I have about five."

Kalo offered me dinner, but I was too tired to eat and just drank tea, while water for a bath was heated on a bucket on the kerosene stove. When it was ready, Kalo carried it around the house and showed me the washtub, next to a faucet from a catchment tank. After carefully rinsing off the worst of the salt, I returned to the house and was given a room where a cot was made up with real sheets. I lay for a few moments in this unaccustomed luxury and thought of CHIDIOCK TICHBORNE drifting somewhere in the night toward Australia.

A little after 7:00 the next morning there was a knock on the door, and a bearded man about my age, wearing black-rimmed glasses, jeans, and a short-sleeved shirt, came in.

"I hope I am not disturbing you." The man held out his hand, both to shake mine and to motion for me to remain in bed. "I am Fred Timakata, the village chief. I am sorry not to have been home when you arrived, but I was meeting with the chiefs of the other villages. How are you feeling?"

"Better, though still tired."

"I troubled you so early because we have a radio schedule with Vila at 8:00 and I am going to ask if they have a plane free. Are there any messages you want to send?"

This was unexpected and welcome news. "You have an airfield?"

"For the past two years. Just a clearing in the bush, but enough for small planes. We have saved many lives by being able to fly people out rather than having to wait for a ship."

I wrote out a telegram for Suzanne. "CHIDIOCK TICHBORNE lost. I fine. At Emae Island, New Hebrides. Will telephone from Port Vila within week."

Fred took the message and started to leave for the island's only school, where the radio transmitter was located. Just before he closed the door, he said, "Oh yes. I have asked the dresser to come by."

To someone more familiar with British usage, his meaning would have been clear, but my speculation as to who or what the 'dresser' might be ended only when a shy young man, carrying a large black bag, knocked on the door and announced, "I am the dresser."

To this I ventured a neutral, "Yes."

"Yes." He held up the bag as a badge of office. "I have come to give you injections."

"For what?"

"To make you well."

"What kind of injections?"

He displayed a bottle of clear fluid.

"And what is that?"

He was surprised I did not recognize it. "Medicine."

"But what kind of medicine?"

"To make you well."

"No."

"But it will make you well."

"No medicine."

Losing such an opportunity was obviously a disappointment and, after a pause, he made another offer. "I will take your blood pressure."

To this I agreed. But when he took out the instrument, it was broken. Desperately he rummaged through the black bag before exclaiming, "I will get you some calamine lotion."

Believing this would cause no harm and seeing how eager he was to do something, I again agreed. Seldom have I made anyone so happy, and the young man sped from the room to fetch the calamine.

Half an hour later he returned and began to dab the pink liquid on my hands and feet. As he worked, we made small talk. I learned that his name was James. He was born on Emae, but trained to be a dresser at a hospital on the big island of Espiritu Santo.

When he was almost finished painting me, he mentioned offhandedly, "Oh, yes. They found your boat."

My words tumbled out, "What? Who? Where?"

Before James could reply, Fred Timakata appeared at the door. "Yes. Your boat was floating upside down in the lagoon at the other end of the island."

This was incredible. When last seen CHIDIOCK TICHBORNE was far to the south of Emae and I had accepted that she was lost.

"Is she badly damaged?"

"Probably so, I'm afraid. After the men from Sangava village saw the boat, they searched the beach for bodies, thinking that it was a lifeboat from a ship. When they came up to the school to report, I told them about you."

My excitement was difficult to contain. "Is the boat still afloat?"

"They said they had dragged it ashore."

"Can we get there?"

"It would be necessary to walk some, but the truck could take us most of the way. When you feel well enough, that is."

"I am well enough now."

"But your feet . . ."

"I must see the boat."

I managed to get thongs salvaged from the swamping partly on my feet and we all climbed into the truck and rolled down the hill and along the jungle track.

After stopping in Sangava as a courtesy to the village chief, and in order to pick up men who knew the boat's exact location, we left the trail and dodged trees until the truck was stopped by thick bush. "We have to walk from here," Fred told me. "They say it is not far."

The Sangava men led us through the vegetation. I could hear the sound of surf, but I did not catch a glimpse of the beach until we actually stepped onto it. My shipwreck was the biggest news on Emae Island since the fighting in Guadalcanal during World War II. In their excitement the men took off down the beach at a pace that soon left me limping far behind. In the distance they joined a group clustered at the edge of the jungle. As I neared, the men quietly stepped aside and there was CHIDIOCK TICHBORNE, not only safe but sound. Her hull was intact. From the gunwale down it was not even scratched. And for the first time since the pitchpole, she was empty of water.

When I later studied a detailed chart of Emae Island, I found notation of a current running clockwise around the offshore rock. CHIDIOCK must have been carried south by this current before being returned to be swept over the reef during the night. She had flipped in the surf. Her mast and gaff were shattered, the heavy bronze stem fitting bent, and the teak gunwale cap splintered near the bow and along the stern. But these were all just pieces to be stuck back on. She almost seemed to have followed me ashore. I half expected her to ask what had taken me so long.

While I was remembering, I had continued to walk and now found myself at the end of Cook's Beach. Other memories returned as I retraced my steps to the house:

My first real meal at Fred's home that Sunday evening: turtle stew, supplied by the islanders, and the treat, for them, of freeze-dried chicken chow mein, supplied by me. My almost regal progress by truck to the airstrip, during which everyone we passed waved or saluted. The efficient British Base Hospital in Port Vila, where I was told by the Australian doctor that coming from a civilized country I had the dubious advantage of having civilized staph, which were resistant to the antibiotics used in the New Hebrides; where one night I awoke from a feverish nightmare, reaching up, trying to strike out at the wave towering over me, only to discover that it was a frightened nurse with my 2:00 a.m. medicine. The old woman who smiled and gently touched my swollen feet and gave me in broken English the ultimate accolade: "You win the big sea." The moment when I was through the barrier at Auckland Airport and held Suzanne.

I climbed the low dune separating the house from the beach and stood there for a moment. A telegram from England, advising me of the shipment of CHIDIOCK TICHBORNE's replacement parts in what would become a race with the cyclone season, had arrived that morning.

9 The Proper Storm

On a moonless night I found sixteen shades of darkness.

Six were in the sky: an over-all blackness of the heavens; a diffuse gray to the west, although the sun had set hours earlier; the pinpricks of the stars; a few scattered shadows that were clouds; the flow of the Milky Way; and sporadic flashes of lightning far to the north.

The sea revealed even less than the sky. It seemed to have turned in upon itself and to be studying its own depths for hidden memories. It breathed with deep, low respirations, in rhythm to a long, low swell from the south. The waves, only inches high and from the east, were a lighter gray than the swell, or, rather, than the back of the swell, for it was not visible until it had passed. The shadows of clouds, shadows of shadows, were impenetrably dark. And there were a few flashes of phosphorescence as CHIDIOCK TICHBORNE ghosted forward.

On CHIDIOCK could be found six more shades. The featureless triangle of the mainsail undulated above me. Around me was an indistinct cockpit. A solid black line marked the teak gunwale's absorption of all light. There were the vaguely golden columns of the varnished masts; lumps of bags; and my own form, clad in foulweather gear.

The foulweather gear was worn not in anticipation of bad weather, but because everything was covered with evening dampness. For me on CHIDIOCK, on even the best of nights, foulweather gear served as pajamas.

I wondered about the impressionists' tenet that all shadows have color. In all that I saw, only a few stars, the masts, and the foulweather gear revealed even subdued color, hidden as though beneath a thousand years of soot. Yet perhaps more color was there.

When I had exhausted these permutations of darkness, my mind moved outward. Darwin lay a week behind; Bali, I hoped, less than a week ahead, although after several fifty-mile days I was not making any predictions. Sometime since leaving Darwin, CHID-IOCK and I had completed ten thousand miles. I was not certain just when. I have never been able to answer when someone asks how many miles I have done. Still, ten thousand miles in an open boat was something of a milestone, and this particular passage was the final phase of the transition that had been taking place since Cairns, Australia. The trade winds and the open Pacific had given way to seas crowded with shipping and dominated by land. Although I did not intend to, it would be possible to sail practically all the way to Gibraltar in sight of land. The thought was appalling. I realized that perhaps only the Pacific and the Southern Ocean are truly open. I already missed the Pacific, even as I was drawn onward by the exotic names appearing on the new charts: Sumbawa, Lombok, Bali, Java.

Darwin had been an unexpectedly good stop. I suppose the impression of Darwin I had before arriving there was based on a photograph of the muddy commercial basin. Actually, the dry season anchorage off the Darwin Sailing Club a couple of miles northwest of the commercial basin is clean, with a good landing on a sand beach, although with twenty-five foot spring tides, boats larger than CHIDIOCK often have to anchor a good half mile off.

A kind of frontier spirit exists in the Northern Territory, as it does in far north Queensland. The people are very friendly, if given to gloating over their weather during the dry season and the June sunsets. Such gloating is justified. In my two visits to Darwin, both during June, about ten drops of rain fell, the humidity was low for the tropics, and the sunsets, caused by dust being blown into the air over the vast desert to the west, are the most consistently spectacular I have found anywhere in the world.

What I like best about Darwin is the wildlife. In a city of more than fifty thousand people, nature has not been subdued. Two-foot long lizards called goannas walk among the tables on the grounds of the Sailing Club. One of these gave me pause when it refused a scrap of a meat pie I was eating. Hawks soar overhead. Dugongs browse through the anchorage. And the occasional crocodile chases someone up the boat-launching ramp.

This new beginning, this departure from the familiar world of Australia en route to the unknown of the East, caused me to recall my departure from San Diego more than two years earlier and to consider what had changed in ten thousand miles. Two things stood out. Now I knew the voyage was possible. The departure from San Diego had been a leap into the unknown, if a calculated one in a tried hull. Viewed objectively after ten thousand miles, the odds of our successfully completing the circumnavigation seemed to me about the same as those for any other boat, although weighted somewhat differently. We might be overwhelmed a bit earlier than some vessels if caught by a storm, but we would better survive the more likely crises, such as going onto a reef.

The other major difference was that when I left San Diego, I did not know if I would see Suzanne again, while now I knew that she would be in Bali on July 3. There was for me great contentment in being able to enjoy solitude at sea and still share harbor life. Sailing CHIDIOCK was a struggle to impose purpose in a medium of chaotic change, although it might not seem so on this smooth night. My feelings for Suzanne were one of the few constants in that chaos. She had shared the limitations of an open boat as a home, reduced her worldly goods to a single duffel bag, learned to cook well on a camp stove, and endured a succession of potentially final farewells. I think it was Winston Churchill who said that his wife was the sheet anchor of his life. That is what Suzanne had become for me.

Other things too had changed in ten thousand miles, but these were only details. I dislike clutter and confusion, and I would like to think I have a talent for finding the simplest way to solve problems, at least on boats. One of the reasons I have been able to keep going so long is because I have kept myself as strong as possible, while making sailing as easy as possible.

As CHIDIOCK slouched along, I thought: Well, if we aren't going very fast, we aren't paying a very high price in wear and tear on boat or crew either. In fact, except for a few mold spores developing in the fresh water supply, we don't really have any problems. I should be and was grateful.

For eleven days and eight hundred miles CHIDIOCK eased her way westward. We did not in that time ship a single wave. In boredom I took many more sights than usual and knew our position with rare precision. I even stopped winding myself into the tarp at night.

Light winds were to be expected during this time of year. Yet I had known passages that began quietly and ended noisily, and was not altogether surprised when on the eleventh day, thick clouds rushed down upon us and rain began to fall. The island of Sumbawa was not far off, but its volcanic peaks, ranging to over 12,000 feet, were hidden by the storm. That night there were not sixteen shades of darkness; there was only one: absolute blackness outside of me matched by absolute blackness within. At 11:00 p.m., instead of rushing blindly on, steering by feel down waves I never saw, I hove to.

We did not resume sailing until 9:00 a.m. the next day, after I had managed to grab three quick sights of a sun indistinct through clouds and over a ragged horizon of eight-foot waves. Usually I would not attempt to use the sextant aboard CHIDIOCK in such conditions, and I was annoyed that, when sights had not been essential, they came easily, but now that I needed them, they did not. Two of the position lines were a mile apart and the third was just eight miles farther east, which I considered acceptable. I concluded that the east end of Lombok was due north of us. Bali was sixty miles west, too far to reach before sunset. I could only hope to get close enough to enter port the following day.

In mid-morning a promontory on Lombok became distinct for a few minutes before being lost in another squall. At sea visibility was improving, with most of the clouds passing harmlessly overhead on their way to loose torrents on the high islands.

For several hours Lombok played hide-and-seek with us, but by 2:00 p.m. I could see enough of the coast to recognize that we were now off the west cape and sailing into a trap. Bali, although still not in view, lay only thirty miles away. In the first ten miles were the swift currents of Lombok Strait, running at up to eight knots. The next ten were bordered by the island of Penida. And then the last ten led to Benoa harbor, on Bali, safety for a vessel once inside but until then a lee shore. It was a box, blocked to the north and west by land, and as effectively to the east by winds of thirty to forty knots. We could still safely escape by reaching off to the southwest, but to do so would be to risk being blown past Bali during the night.

The little yawl dashed on while I considered unappealing alternatives. When 1,700 feet high Penida came into sight at 3:00 p.m., I turned CHIDIOCK into the wind and hove to under mizzen alone.

We were making stern way directly onto the island, which I estimated to be about eight miles distant. Even at just one knot we would be on it during the night, and if this night was to be as black as the previous one, we could not afford to get too close. For the moment, though, we were safe, and it seemed odd to be hove to during daylight.

I sat in the cockpit for a while, trying to judge our rate of drift. In an hour, Penida definitely drew closer, but not as rapidly as I had feared. So on the assumption that somehow we would reach Benoa safely, I took this opportunity to wash myself and to shave.

As sunset neared I managed to heat a package of freeze-dried beef stew, but I could not succeed in brewing a cup of tea.

The view to windward was not promising. Heavy clouds showed no sign of clearing. The view to leeward was not promising. Individual trees on Penida were distinct. I stared broodingly to the southwest. That way was still open. We could reach off now. Sooner or later this storm would end and we would wind up somewhere. I imagined Suzanne's reaction if after being in Bali for several days, she received a telegram from me in Java. Thoughts, calculations, plans, worries, fears, balanced one another, and I finally did nothing. We would be all right until at least 10:00 p.m. In the meantime I would try to sleep.

A few minutes after I covered myself with the tarp, three waves hit us. The first caught CHIDIOCK abeam and threw her sideways in a great blast of spray; the second seemed to take her from below and toss her into the air, like a juggler; and the third came from ahead, lifting the bow until the little yawl seemed in danger of performing her first backwards somersault. I pulled the tarp away and began pumping the bilge.

Although we were west of the strongest currents through Lombok Strait, we were obviously in the midst of a battle between strong wind and strong current. These were the conditions we had found several weeks earlier near Cape York, here greatly magnified. Ten-foot waves leapt up all around us, fell, smashed into one another, rebounded, reformed, and broke again.

I was more angry than frightened. Of all the miserable places to have to heave to, I thought. The jagged waves cast long shadows in the fading light. The air temperature was tropical, but I felt cold, as though CHIDIOCK were being tossed about among frozen mountain peaks. The way to the southwest seemed ever more inviting, but I did nothing except sit and wait; and when after fifteen minutes no other waves repeated the assault of the first three, I lay back, pulled the slimy tarp over my head, and again tried to sleep.

Unexpectedly, sleep came. There was no reason for me to be especially tired. Until the day before, I had been as comfortable aboard CHIDIOCK as I would have been in harbor, yet I found myself dreaming. A sea snake, such as I had often seen in northern Australian waters, had been washed into CHIDIOCK and I kept trying to hit him with an oar, but I was able to move only in slow motion and the snake kept slithering away. In the dream CHIDIOCK became a long marble corridor, down which I endlessly pursued the snake. After forty-five minutes of this restful pastime, I awoke. Night was complete. Penida had disappeared. But from the west came a faint loom of light, the first sign of Bali.

I returned to sleep, but throughout the night I awoke at thirty to forty-five minute intervals. The result was a wide range of dreams, but at least the sea snake did not reappear.

When I decided to hold our position and await developments, I had hoped that the sky might clear or the wind decrease or the seas diminish or CHIDIOCK's angle of drift change so that we would miss Penida. Any one of these would have been enough, and the third or fourth time I awoke, I realized that just as CHIDIOCK is a self-simplifying boat, so this night, which had threatened to become an ordeal, had turned into a self-solving problem. Half the sky was clear, and in the starlight, Penida lay safely north of us. The wind had dropped below twenty knots, the seas to around five feet. I permitted myself a smile. Sometimes it really does happen. You lie down and cover your head and it all goes away. My awakening at short intervals continued, but was unnecessary, for conditions only continued to improve. Not long after midnight, I could see the revolving beacon at Benoa Harbor.

The next morning was sunny and warm, with such light wind for a while that I began to be concerned that we might yet be carried south of Bali by currents.

By 10:00 a.m. we were only two miles offshore and I caught a glimpse of patches of white in the distance, which I thought at first were waves breaking against a cliff. Only as we drew closer could I see that they were sails and that the sea was full of them, inverted triangles of multicolored cloth on *gujungs*, the local one-man fishing craft, which darted about like swift water spiders.

On the chart Benoa appears easy to find; it is the first opening in the coast north of the south end of Bali. But soon I began to wonder. A new set of clouds was spreading rapidly over the sky; the wind had increased to fifteen knots; and the storm appeared to be preparing for Act Two by washing all color from sea, land, and sky, and repainting everything a uniform gun-metal gray.

The fishing boats, which were south of me, began speeding home. As the first of them neared, I could see the fishermen, wearing long-sleeved shirts, long pants, and conical bamboo hats. Hand lines trailed from reels in the sterns of their small trimarans. The vessels' narrow centerhulls and bamboo outriggers were well maintained and decorated with colorful designs.

The *gujungs* easily outsailed CHIDIOCK, then making six knots, and the first twenty or so confused me by continuing beyond a break in the palm trees that I thought led to Benoa.

Boat after boat streamed past, with another fleet running before a black line squall to the west, and all of them sailed determinedly north.

I let CHIDIOCK close with the coast until we were only a few hundred yards beyond what was definitely the first opening in the shore. It gave no other sign of being a harbor. I could see no ships inside. And the waves on the reef seemed to be breaking solidly.

Another group of *gujungs* approached. I backed the jib and let CHIDIOCK forereach across their course. Clutching the mizzen mast, I stood and pointed toward the shore, "Benoa?" I yelled about the rising wind.

The nearest fisherman pointed with an oval loaf of bread he had been eating from one hand while steering with the other. From my perspective I could not tell whether he was pointing in or up the coast. "Benoa?" I repeated. But he had already turned away and the reply came from a second fisherman, who, as he whizzed by, gestured for me to follow. By now I could see that several of the boats were almost to the surf. I re-trimmed the jib and trailed after them.

With the boats of the fishing fleet showing the way as they passed us on both sides, finding the channel was not difficult. It involved a starboard broad reach followed by a gybe to a port broad reach. The surf appeared to be solid because the reef from the north overlaps the reef from the south.

Rain was falling heavily on the land and behind us at sea. The *gujungs* were bright jewels against dark velvet. Some of the fishermen smiled, some made shy hand motions that might have been meant in greeting, some stared at me curiously, and most ignored me. Finally one called in English, "Where you from?" Thinking that California was too far, I settled for "Darwin." He looked surprised, then grinned and gave me a thumbs up.

By the time I was off Benoa's fishing village, the first of the *gujungs* had already been pulled above the high-tide mark on the beach. Larger native sailing craft lay at anchor inside the harbor. An intricate Hindu statue stood beneath palm trees. Flute music came from somewhere. There were the smells of fish and spice. Sailing in with the fishing fleet had been beautiful. We had reached the East.

The Red Sea Backwards

Arabia looks just as I expected. The western deserts of America disappoint me because they are not truly barren; almost everywhere something is growing. But Arabia has the terrible beauty of pure desolation—sand and rock, brown mountains rising inland, medieval forts on two of the hills near Bab el Mandeb, the southern entrance to the Red Sea, through which we had passed the preceding afternoon, a cluster of huts in a fishing village, and that is truly all.

The sea turned bright green and flat on our second day out of Aden, which I had left after only four days of rest following the forty-seven-day, four-thousand-mile nonstop passage from Singapore, the longest open boat passage I, or anyone else, ever made. I had learned that my grandmother, my only relative, was dying in California, and I was trying to get the boat to Port Sudan, where I could leave it and fly back.

For two hours CHIDIOCK sped north. At noon, when we were off a village called Dhubab, she began speeding too fast, skating on the edge of control at better than seven knots. I furled the mizzen. A few minutes later I reefed the main. We now had only seventy square feet of sail set. A few minutes later, I untied the jib sheet from the tiller and began to steer myself. The easy part of the passage was over. The hard part, in which we would have gale-force winds blowing beneath a hard blue sky for three days, followed by a full week of flat calm in which we made only one hundred and seventy-five miles, the worst I have ever done in any boat, had begun.

Sailing was exciting at first that afternoon as we raced along beside the barren shore. The wind blew steadily, rather than in gusts, and the sea remained smooth. But as the hours and miles passed and the Red Sea began to widen, short, steep waves typical of shallow water began to form. The main shipping route, which had been well to the west of us, began to converge with our course in order to clear a group of islands forty miles to the north. And the wind increased to forty knots.

At 6:00 p.m., keeping one hand on the tiller, I reached back with the other and undid the shock cord on the mizzen. I was not trying to set more sail, but preparing to heave to. When the mizzen was flattened amidships, I spun CHIDIOCK'S bow up into the wind and scrambled for the main halyard. Before I could clear it from the be-laying pin, the wildly flailing sail wrapped the mainsheet around the tiller. The sail filled, turning us dangerously beam on to the seas. Two waves crashed aboard. Then the halyard came free, the gaff slid down, order was restored.

In complete darkness I spooned uncooked freeze-dried chicken stew into my mouth and contemplated our situation. We were about equidistant from the light of the town of Al Mukha to the east and the running lights of ships to the west. Each was about five miles away. The sea itself was not threatening. CHIDIOCK was riding the waves safely; but she was going backwards too fast. Judging our speed was difficult. I thought it might be as much as two knots. If it was, we would cover more than twenty miles before first light and risk being driven ashore or into the midst of the shipping, which was even heavier here than we had seen in the Strait of Malacca. The running lights of at least half a dozen ships were always in view.

For several hours I dozed fitfully as we proceeded stern first up the Red Sea. At 3:00 a.m. something undefinable made me certain that we were about to be driven ashore. I could see nothing except the distant lights of Al Mukha to the south. Conditions were far from suitable for sailing, but I felt we had to try to claw offshore.

There was a moment of transition between being hove to and sailing when CHIDIOCK was out of control. The instant I eased the mizzen sheet, the bow began to swing off the wind, and I aided its momentum by unfurling the jib. Everything seemed to be all right, until I put the tiller amidships and CHIDIOCK gybed. I pulled the tiller hard to starboard and we gybed back, the sails cracking like gunshots as they refilled. I moved the tiller amidships again. Again we gybed and rolled beam onto the waves. I gybed back. More gunshots, more groans from CHIDIOCK'S simple rigging. I could not understand what was happening. Had waves caught us and forced the stern around? Was something wrong with the rudder?

As we surfed down waves I could not see, I experimented with the tiller which was hard over to starboard; when it approached 20°

of amidships, the sails threatened to gybe. Neutral helm was so far to starboard that I could not steer from the port side of the cockpit.

For an hour we thrashed our way northwest. Normally one would speak of thrashing to windward; but although our erratic course, caused by the strange angle of the tiller and my inability to feel or see the following seas, was a broad reach, we seemed to be fighting against the waves rather than moving with them. I was using the bilge pump as much as if we were beating. At 4:00 a.m. I decided that land would not be a threat before dawn, so I again hove to.

I did not attempt to sleep, but sat huddled in the cockpit, worrying about when this wind would decrease and wondering what was wrong with the rudder.

As the sun's first rays flowed over the mountains of Arabia, I saw that the waves had doubled in height during the night, and now ranged up to eight feet. My first reaction was that I was crazy to try to sail in such conditions. I wondered if it would it have been better to have been driven ashore. I was positive we had been in danger.

The rudder was a galvanized steel plate welded to a galvanized steel shaft and could be lifted up into the cockpit from its slot. I had twice bent the rudder shaft on coral, once near Tahiti and once off northern Australia.

Trusting the mizzen and centerboard to keep CHIDIOCK's bow to the wind, I untied the tiller and tried to pull the rudder up, but it would not come. I did not know if the shaft was bent or if the blade was not aligned with the slot. I tried to duplicate the angle at which the tiller had been placed to achieve neutral helm during the night. Bracing myself against the yawl's bobbing and rolling, I pulled, heard the thunk as the rudder blade caught on the hull, moved the tiller another inch to starboard, and pulled again. Finally I found the correct angle, and to my great relief the rudder came up.

The tiller was attached to the rudder by a cap held by a set screw and a tightening screw. The fit was so tight that the cap had to be hammered into place, and this cap had been on the rudder for a year, so it was corroded in place as well. To remove a cap usually took me at least an hour. But one of the waves during the night had thrown us backwards hard enough to loosen this one. I re-aligned and re-tightened the screws and lowered the rudder. Then I sat, feeling cold and wishing the wind would decrease long enough for me to light the stove for a hot cup of coffee, and waited to see what the day would bring.

By noon our situation was becoming untenable. The wind had increased again. I now estimated it as being about fifty knots. The seas had increased to ten or twelve feet, with higher sets coming through at irregular intervals. Even ships, several of which left the shipping channel to investigate CHIDIOCK, were making heavy work of it.

With the increase in force the wind had veered a point to the southwest and was again driving us onto the land. We had drifted past several islands during the morning. Now the largest and northernmost, Jabal Zuqar, was a mile to the west. The island is 2,000 feet high, but has no anchorage. I thought it might at least provide some shelter in its lee. Even more than the previous night, these were not sailing conditions for CHIDIOCK. But we had to try to get away from the Arabian peninsula and possibly even across the shipping route before nightfall.

I tried sailing under jib alone, but the yawl handled better when I set the mizzen as well. The lee of Jabal Zuqar turned out to be an illusion. Steering demanded both hands on the tiller. Wave after wave roared up and threatened to swamp us. Waves smashed into the cliffs of the island, sending spray high into the air, as further east they broke over the bows of southbound ships.

My belief that CHIDIOCK was safe as long as we had sea room and/or I was at the tiller was dealt two severe blows by the Red Sea. The first came in the form of a wave that partially capsized us even though I saw it coming, felt it, and fought it.

That wave struck at about 4:00 p.m. By the time I had pumped CHIDIOCK out, it was 4:30; I decided enough was enough and remained hove to. Our efforts to get offshore had been partially successful. Jabal Zuqar was southeast of us. The wind had backed again to the south. According to the compass, we were drifting backwards on course 350°. Tonight's threat would be shipping.

After forcing down another dinner of uncooked freeze-dried food, I settled in to wait out the miserable night. I was wet, and colder than I had been at sea for several years. I recalled hearing over the transistor radio a week earlier of 50°F temperatures in the

Persian Gulf. I had never thought of cold as being a problem in the Red Sea, although I had lived close enough to deserts to know that they cool off at night. My arms and shoulders and neck were stiff from steering all afternoon. It was, of course, far too wet to take the radio from its protective bag. I watched the running lights of the ships a few miles away and thought of an old sailor's poem:

Western wind, when wilt thou blow,
That the small rain down can rain?
Oh, that my love were in my arms
And I in my bed again.

I didn't want a west wind, but the love and bed would have been most welcome.

I slept sitting up so that I would be able to react quickly. For several hours we seemed to be paralleling the shipping route. At 2:00 a.m. a sound awoke me. I opened my eyes and saw what at first I mistook for a row of street lamps. Perhaps I was just so tired that fear could not touch me. Calmly I thought: Those can't be street lamps. But then, what are they? Not even when I realized that they were the interior lights of a ship did I become upset. Her hull loomed less than ten yards away. I was so close that I could not see the bow, but the knowledge that it would have hit us before I had awakened only added to my fatalistic detachment. Close, but no cigar. I watched with interest as the stern passed and the ship plowed on into the night. And then I closed my eyes and went promptly back to sleep.

I rather expected to wake up and find that the gale had blown itself out. This was March 1 and we were beyond 15°N, the usual limit for gales at that time of year. But it was not to be. The wind was still blowing between forty and fifty knots; the waves were still on average more than ten feet high. The only difference was that they were now smashing a group of rocks called Jaza'ir az Zubayr, to the east of us, instead of into islands to the west as they had been the day before.

These rocks provided some interesting information. One of them was shown on the chart to be one hundred feet high. Spray from breaking waves reached two-thirds of the way up that rock. And it took us just forty-six minutes to drift stern first the two miles that separated two other rocks, giving us a speed of better than 2 1/2 knots. In fact, we were averaging closer to three knots, covering seventy miles a day backwards.

If we had been unlucky to be caught by this gale, we had been lucky to be ten yards west of the ship last night, and lucky again to drift past these rocks at a distance of a few hundred yards without having to try to sail.

The Jaza'ir az Zubayr rocks were the last obstacles for more than sixty miles. The ships had disappeared, presumably somewhere to the west of us. All morning we remained hove to, speeding north stern first. The gale was bad, but I found myself thinking that I was much more tired than I ought to be. Obviously I had not had time to recover in Aden from the almost two months at sea across the Indian Ocean.

At 2:00 p.m. the first of a series of big waves capsized us. Before CHIDIOCK could rise from lying on her beam, a second wave threw her backwards. I clung to the starboard gunwale as though hanging onto the side of a cliff and watched in awe as the ocean creamed through the submerged port half of the cockpit and clutched at my feet. Again, if we had been unlucky to be caught by those waves, we were lucky that the yawl did not dip her masts into the water, for they would surely have been torn away.

When the wave finally released us, tossing us aside like a toy with which it had become bored, CHIDIOCK dropped back onto her bottom. It took a minute or two for me to establish that, incredibly, we were all right. Only the flotation cushions, one bucket, and a chart had been lost. The bucket bobbed nearby. The cushions, one bright red, the other bright yellow, remained visible on distant crests until long after I had bailed and pumped the cockpit dry.

That night the wind finally began to ease, but one more wave partially capsized us. Swimming in the cockpit, I grabbed a bucket and emptied the boat without ever fully waking up.

Tuesday dawn found us hove to against a south wind. Tuesday dusk found us hove to against a north wind. And then we were becalmed for a week. On the other side of the world my grandmother died.

11 *The Island That Would Not Be Passed*

Thinking about it afterwards I succumb to the pathetic fallacy and say that the island waited, for that is the way it seems; that the island was waiting, wreathed in clouds and absolute assurance that she would draw me to her.

To me in Portugal the island was nothing more than an inverted teardrop, marked on the chart of the North Atlantic Ocean, Southern Part, as rising almost 8,000 feet above sea level some seven hundred miles to the southwest, and a guidebook photograph of stone steps leading up to a Spanish church before a backdrop of green mountains. An outpost, the island was the last speck of land off Africa. Beyond it lay nothing but open ocean to the Caribbean. I knew that there was a harbor on the east coast of the island at a place called Santa Cruz. But that was all. I did not need to know more because I had no intention of going there.

Thinking about it afterwards I realize how my life has turned at places I never intended to visit: New Zealand, Vanuatu, Saudi Arabia. Soon it would again—this time at La Palma in the Canary Islands.

In making an Atlantic crossing from Europe to the Caribbean, sailors balance the hurricane season, which ends at the beginning of November, with the advent of winter gales. The accepted rule is to sail down to the Canaries and then wait until January for the trade winds to establish themselves fully. But it was my intention to cross the Atlantic twice that season, sailing CHIDIOCK TICHBORNE II to Antigua and then flying back and sailing RESURGAM, which I had bought earlier that year, across. So I left Portugal in October in CHIDIOCK, despite an unfavorable forecast and early in a season during a year when the world's weather was abnormal almost everywhere.

The wind headed us on the fourth day, ending what had been pleasant though cool sailing. Just after taking a noon sight of a sullen sun lurking behind thin clouds, I changed from sheet-to-tiller self-steering used on a reach to simply tying down the tiller for going to windward. Within a few hours the wind had increased to over twenty knots. The mainsail was reefed. I was perched on the windward seat. Heavy water was breaking over the bow. Alternately pumping and trying to wipe the spray from my eyeglasses, I watched great thunderheads tower above us.

At sunset we were heading directly for a dark purple line squall. Anxiously I scanned the horizon, seeking a way to avoid it. But even as I watched, it grew and advanced upon us. I lowered the mainsail and sat wrapped in the tarp as cold rain plucked inquisitively at my foulweather gear. After an hour, still in the rain, I turned on the flashlight and fumbled through the food bag until I found a can of ravioli, which I ate cold and diluted by rain and salt spray before lying down and trying to sleep.

Under jib and mizzen CHIDIOCK was heeled 15° to port, and it felt as though every wave would capsize her. I did not expect that under those conditions she would capsize; it just felt that way. I lay down and pulled the tarp over my head and tried to tuck it in at the side and over my feet. I knew that I would not sleep, but there was nothing else to do.

I screamed at the sky.

That first gale lasted two days and three longer nights. During the second night the wind increased to over fifty knots and I had no choice but to heave to for five hours, during which we were driven backwards at three knots, or three times faster than our velocity-made-good of one knot earlier in the day.

I accepted that storm. I had set sail knowing of the low near Madeira. I had expected it to move, but obviously it had not. So I had gambled and lost and had to take the consequences. On the third morning the wind gradually weakened, the black waves began to average less than ten feet, and the sky partially cleared. By afternoon, puffy, regularly spaced, low, white clouds and a northeast breeze made me wonder if we were already on the edge of the trades. If so, the gale had been a fair price.

After the poor sailing in the Red Sea and the Mediterranean, I let my mind recall fine fast days in the Bay of Bengal and the Coral Sea. I was looking forward to this last ocean passage, to giving CHIDIOCK her head and letting her dash off in a series of one hundred mile days. Perhaps we could challenge our best runs ever. After three times making more than one hundred and forty miles in twenty-four hours, this would be our last chance to try to break one hundred and fifty, for good sailing could not be expected from the Caribbean back to San Diego. All this I contemplated because of a few puffy white clouds. How adaptable is man, which is to say how easily does he deceive himself.

By nature I am an optimist, by experience a pessimist. Experience won again. At sunset we were sailing directly for a dark purple line squall. I did not scream at the sky because of that. I screamed because the wind had returned to the southwest, again directly heading us. I informed the sky that if we had to have another gale, at least I was entitled to a reaching gale. The sky ignored me. Except for a few hours, CHIDIOCK TICHBORNE II would never know reaching conditions again.

Ahead of us, beyond that wind, now two hundred miles closer, Atlantic waves smashed into the black volcanic rocks of La Palma Island.

A kind of madness comes to a sailor in a small boat in a gale, if by madness one means the acceptance as normal of conditions that are far from acceptable. That night I slept for twenty minutes when I first lay down at 7:00 p.m., but I lay wet and shivering beneath the tarp until almost dawn before sleep came to me again.

As CHIDIOCK slammed and slithered through a pitch-black night, the pitiful barriers between my body and the sea were breached. Hull, tarp, foulweather gear, clothes, were useless in this second gale, which struck before I had dried out from the first. The dividing line that night between myself and the ocean became very thin.

The struggle was unceasing. Lying down, my cold wet shirt plastered against my back beneath wet foulweather gear, my cold wet jeans plastered against my legs, my cold wet feet inside wet plastic bags, I snaked an arm from the tarp and pumped the bilge every few minutes. I tried to count the strokes but lost track at more than two hundred when CHIDIOCK lurched. There must have been thousands of strokes every hour, hour after hour. I reached the mainsheet. This was what made me think of madness. Teetering always on the verge of burying the lee gunwale and swamping, at intervals CHIDIOCK started actually to go over, and I did not even bother to sit up but just reached out blindly and played the main-sheet as one would a racing dinghy around the buoys in a harbor. A sailor does not live on or even in a boat as small as Chidiock; he wears her. Truly I was at one with my ship.

Conditions were such that I knew that were I living ashore I would not go daysailing even on a larger boat. Deliberately I turned my mind away, as one might from a battlefield, and tried to think of something more pleasant. But while my mind wandered, my arm continued to play the mainsheet.

Within a few hours the wind decreased to less than twenty knots and we had more reasonable sailing. The 12,172 feet high volcanic peak of Tenerife Island appeared twenty miles or so to the south.

That night I slept well. We were becalmed.

For three days we drifted off Tenerife and celebrated two anniversaries: November 11, my forty-second birthday; and November 12, the fifth anniversary of the beginning of this voyage.

For my birthday, Chidiock presented me with a broken shroud. On a larger boat this would have been serious, but on the yawl I was able to lower the mast and tie a jury-rigged line to replace the wire, which had snapped at a swage.

Fluky afternoon breezes enabled us to make a few miles each day. On the afternoon of the twelfth, the shadow that was La Palma Island appeared on the horizon southwest of us. I considered if I should put in for provisions. This was our fourteenth day at sea, and we had covered only seven hundred miles. Chidiock had been provisioned in Portugal for two months, but we still had two thousand seven hundred miles to go. If we ever found the trades, we would have no problem. But if we continued to make only fifty miles a day, I would soon have to start rationing supplies, which, unrationed, hardly provided a luxurious diet.

I glanced at my face in the mirror. A bit gaunt. I pinched my arm, like a housewife testing a chicken in a store. A bit stringy. But I supposed that losing a few more pounds would not kill me.

A return of wind, from the southwest naturally, was followed by the obligatory sunset line squall. The north end of La Palma Island lay roughly five miles south of us when the black clouds came together with a sound of thunder, which might as well have been the slamming shut of a door to the open ocean forever.

Quickly the wind rose above forty knots. For CHIDIOCK these were conditions in which to heave to, but I wanted desperately to get past the island. I tried to stagger on under jib and mizzen. Initially I held the tiller in my right hand and played the jib sheet with my left to keep from capsizing. But soon I could not hold the thirty-square-foot sail with my left hand and had to switch to my right. CHIDIOCK toppled from crest to trough, her gunwale scooped up the ocean, solid water covered the bow. Above the sound of the crashing water came a high-pitched whine from the rigging.

The strain on hull and rig and sailor was immense. I knew that we should not be sailing, that despite all the commotion, we really weren't getting anywhere. CHIDIOCK simply did not have the weight to carry forward motion through such waves. We were actually leaping up and down in one place, making at most a knot and not even in the desired direction. At least, or so I told myself, we were not losing miles.

Yet we were not to be permitted even that solace. After an hour the wind increased to the point where I could not control the jib sheet with both hands while trying to steer with my knee. We had no choice but to heave to. I reached for the jib-furling line and pulled on it with one hand while slackening the jib sheet with the other. The sail flogged dreadfully, shaking the rig, the hull, me, trying to tear us apart. The furling line came taut. The sail still flogged. CHIDIOCK was out of control.

Thinking that either the furling line had snarled on the drum or that the head swivel had jammed, I tried to ease the line. The full sail flogged harder and pushed the boat stern first into a wave that broke over us. CHIDIOCK shook herself free from most of the water, but the cockpit remained partially full. I tried the furling line again. Again it came taut with the sail only partially furled.

With water in the cockpit acting as ballast, the little yawl settled somewhat. 'Settled' is an ominous word. From the tiller I grabbed a couple of shockcords normally used for self-steering and waded forward. My weight on the bow reduced our inches of freeboard dangerously, but when I captured and tied the flogging sail, the mizzen took control and relative order was restored.

By the time I had pumped out the cockpit, the squall had passed and a few stars were peering shyly through the clouds. I found the flashlight and tried to figure out what was wrong with the jib. In reduced winds, I experimentally unfurled and furled the sail until I realized that when I had replaced the furling line after jury-rigging the shroud that had broken earlier, I had put enough wraps on the drum to furl the sail completely in normal wind, but the tension on the sail in whatever wind we had just been through had caused the sail to wrap so much tighter that half of it remained exposed.

This was a fortunate discovery, for it prevented me from resuming sailing until I had crawled forward and put additional wraps on the drum. Before I finished, another squall hit, and we remained hove to.

There is an immense difference between trying to beat against a gale and being hove to. For several hours I actually slept fairly well in at least fifty knots of wind. Only occasionally did a wave leap aboard. Only occasionally did I have to pump. CHIDIOCK rode the waves like the proverbial cork.

The problem was that we were going too quickly in the wrong direction, as I knew from the storm in the Red Sea when I made more than two hundred miles stern first while hove to for three days. At 1:00 a.m. I saw from the compass that the wind had shifted to the northwest. By playing with the mizzen sheet and centerboard, I was able to change our drift to the south. During the hours we had already been hove to we must have been pushed safely away from La Palma, I reasoned. The island is about twenty miles long, running north/south. Thinking that if we could not get past the north end of the island, perhaps this gale would push us past the south, I went back to sleep.

The sky was clear of all but a few distant clouds. The sun was bright, the waves slight. I had set the jib and resumed sailing before dawn. Now CHIDIOCK sat under full sail. The white buildings of Santa Cruz dotted the shore a few miles west of us. I watched cars climb a road clinging to the steep, rocky shore. I watched Iberia 727s land and take off from a runway carved from those cliffs. I gazed up at the green peaks, rising behind the city, just as they had in the almost forgotten guidebook photograph. I did all this at some length that Sunday morning. We were becalmed.

Across smooth water, CHIDIOCK raced for the last rock off the south end of La Palma. Ahead of us the open Atlantic sparkled in the sunlight. The wind had returned just after noon on Sunday.

Sitting on the starboard cockpit seat, I was content. CHIDIOCK TICHBORNE II was still hard on the wind, the tiller tied down, the jury-rigged shroud to weather, but she was dancing along at five knots. This was the first fine sailing of the passage. I expected to put La Palma behind us before sunset.

When that last rock was still three miles away, another door slammed, though this time without a drumroll of thunder. From a clear sky, the wind increased to gale force. Even close to shore the sea became choppy. CHIDIOCK's speed dropped; her bow fell off until she was pointing due south toward the island of Hierro, thirty miles away.

For a while I let the boat head that way, hoping that we would work clear of what might be only a locally strong wind funneling around high land. Yet the farther south we sailed, the stronger the wind blew. I glanced back north. The sea was covered with white-caps to the horizon. On our present heading we would have to pass east of Hierro sometime during the night, but if we turned, we would have a reach back to the north end of La Palma. CHIDIOCK would make at least six knots reaching in this wind. I untied the tiller, and we came about.

That afternoon was splendid—a last hurrah, although I did not know it then. CHIDIOCK remained well balanced under jib and mizzen. Out of pleasure rather than necessity, I kept the helm in warm sunshine. The low waves pushed us rather than stopped us. CHIDIOCK seemed to enjoy the romp.

The rock at the south end of La Palma quickly disappeared. The white buildings of Santa Cruz passed abeam yet again. A rock at the north end of the island came into view. I expected to have a late dinner, for I had decided to continue steering until we were past the island, but I did not expect it to be as late as it was.

The wind disappeared with the sinking sun. Twilight found me playing cat's-paws, trying to crawl the last mile to a flashing navigation beacon. This time the door closed silently. Between 6:00 p.m. and 7:00 p.m. we made two hundred yards, and I gave the wind an ultimatum: Either let us pass the light by 8:00 or I will go into Santa

Cruz to reprovision, perhaps re-rig, rest, and wait for the weather to improve.

At 8:00 p.m. the light insolently flashed half a mile to our west. A glassy sea reflected stars. CHIDIOCK drifted quietly. No breath of wind troubled the flame of the stove as I heated water for a cup of tea. I tried to turn the bow toward oft-passed Santa Cruz.

It was the middle of the following morning before I reached the breakwater, behind which I found a small, rather dirty harbor filled with a few small freighters, about twenty yachts, all sensibly waiting for a break in the weather, and some fishing boats. The freighters were tied to a wharf at the north end of the harbor, near the center of the town. The yachts were anchored off a high cliff to which they had run stern lines. On the top of that cliff, reached by stone steps, sat the Club Náutico. The fishing boats were on moorings near the south end of the harbor, beneath a several hundred foot high cliff. A forlorn arc of black sand ran between this cliff and the lower one at the Club Náutico. The beach seemed to be composed more of cinders than of sand.

Having lowered the sails, I kept CHIDIOCK stationary with the oars and considered where to put her. Clouds began pouring over the mountains, blotting out the sun. Gusts of wind scurried about the harbor. I let them push us closer to the yachts. A woman rowed out from one of them. Some men standing near the fishing boats yelled something and gestured toward a vacant mooring. As she came within hailing distance, the woman said, "Webb Chiles, I presume." I cannot pretend not to be pleased at being recognized. Her name was Annie. She asked where I had come from. I asked what the weather had been like in the harbor and in what depth the yachts were anchored. As we drifted I saw that there really was no room for me among the other yachts. Of course, there was space for the hull, but not enough for CHIDIOCK to move about as much as she likes, even if I put a stern line ashore.

I rowed toward the mooring indicated by the men ashore. CHIDIOCK was much smaller than the fishing boats; presumably what held them would hold her. I could always move later.

I took the mooring, tying fore and aft to it as the nearby fishing boats were tied. I waved my thanks to the men ashore, who smiled and waved back. A sheet of hard rain drove Annie back to her boat, the men ashore into a shack, and me hurriedly to erect CHIDIOCK's harbor tarp/tent. That we were deep in the shadow of the cliff did not seem significant.

In Portugal I had met a beautiful English woman, whom I telephoned and asked to come out and spend a few days with me. The forecast was for continued unsettled weather, so I wasn't going anywhere for a while. She agreed, but her travel agent in London had only a vague concept of the Canary Islands and put her on a flight to Lanzarote, the island closest to Africa and furthest from La Palma. I got on one of the 727s I had watched from the sea and flew to spend some time on Lanzarote.

The Iberia jet banked slowly on the approach. During the short flight from Tenerife on that lovely sunny morning, I was pleased to see a sparkling ocean touched by a light easterly wind. Perfect sailing conditions. I went over the list of things I had to do before setting off across the Atlantic. Mostly it was just re-provisioning and re-packing everything in plastic bags.

It was Thursday, November 24, 1983. I had been away from La Palma for a week, longer than expected because a storm had shut down the airport at Tenerife, through which I had to fly to and from Lanzarote. In high spirits, with no sense of foreboding, I paid the taxi driver and walked through the Club Náutico to the patio overlooking the almost deserted harbor. Most of the yachts had already taken advantage of the fine weather and left for the Caribbean. CHIDIOCK TICHBORNE II was not there either.

For a moment I thought I was not looking in the right place, that the little yawl must be behind one of the fishing boats. I walked to the end of the wall. She was not on any of the moorings. My eyes swept the beach. I could not see her anywhere.

I called down to the crew of a catamaran who were preparing to weigh anchor. They called back something that I could not understand and pointed toward a launching ramp near the fishing boats. I followed their arms and saw CHIDIOCK's hull sitting there without masts.

I found my inflatable and learned from various people that the storm which had closed the airport on Tenerife had brought hurricane force winds to La Palma. The gusts were strongest beneath the cliff. In one of them CHIDIOCK capsized. Fishermen managed to get her ashore. The authorities had taken everything removable, including the masts, to the marine headquarters for safe keeping, but before they had done so, someone had broken into the only locker and stolen some equipment.

I rowed to the ramp and walked up to CHIDIOCK. As always she had survived. Other than the deliberately smashed locker latch, the only damage was two broken belaying pins. The oversized padlock lay locked on the cockpit floor.

I went to the marine headquarters and was sympathetically shown the equipment and stores being kept by them. A good many things had been lost when the boat turned over: provisions, charts, a compass, anchors, clothing. Other necessities, including my sextant, which was in the locked locker, had been stolen.

Those losses completed a process begun by a capsize in the Pacific in 1978. I did not own anything—not a single article of clothing, not a book, not a cassette, not a chart, not a radio or a sextant or a camera, not a teaspoon—that I had owned when I left San Diego on November 12, 1978. It is just as well that possessions do not matter, for they do not survive a voyage in an open boat.

I thanked the men and crossed the street to the Club Náutico, where I stood for only a few moments, looking out at the sea on which CHIDIOCK TICHBORNE I and II and I had sailed twenty-five thousand miles. There was not the slightest sign we had ever been there. Putting the boat and the voyage back together again would not be difficult. It would take nothing more than some time and some money. But I knew that I would not do it. Someone later said how disheartening that moment must have been. It was not in the slightest. Almost a decade earlier, having to turn away from Cape Horn because of rigging damage was disheartening. A year earlier, losing CHIDIOCK TICHBORNE I to Saudi officialdom and being divorced from Suzanne was disheartening. Almost a decade later, losing RESURGAM and Jill within a few hours, was disheartening. There are more circles in my life than those I have carved on the world's oceans with boats. I glanced at my watch. I had been back on the island barely an hour. I turned and walked away.

Three months and an ocean distant, I found myself considering that decision aboard RESURGAM in English Harbour, Antigua. I had waited to be certain I had not been precipitous. Despite occasional slight twinges—it would have been pleasant to have had both boats together there, living aboard RESURGAM, gunkholing in CHIDIOCK—I never had any serious regrets.

Although there was some public interest, I made the voyage to please myself, and I stopped for the same reason. I had started the voyage to sail to the edge of human experience, to explore the unknown, to try to do what some people considered to be impossible. After five years and twenty-five thousand miles, that edge of experience had been charted, that unknown had become known, that impossible proved possible. I had nothing more to learn from it; and I was no longer willing to subordinate everything in my life to it. I had long since surpassed what other men had done, and for years had only been competing with myself.

It was evening. I made myself a vodka and tonic, sans ice, and sat in the cockpit, watching pelicans hunt through the twilight. For a moment I wondered what the open boat voyage meant. I did not know. As the dying replicant said in the movie *Blade Runner*, "I have seen things that you cannot even imagine. But all these memories will be lost in time as tears are lost in rain." Perhaps it meant nothing and life is merely an unknown voyage from mystery to mystery. But I am glad I made it.

PART III

RESURGAM

RESURGAM was also a stock British boat, a She 36, designed by the American firm of Sparkman and Stevens. When I bought her in 1983, the dollar was strong versus the pound sterling, making boats atypically much less expensive in England than the U.S.

She was my first used boat, but not my last. The spread between new and used boat prices has increased dramatically and, at least for me, decisively during the past decade.

She was similar to EGREGIOUS, a 1970's IOR racer, with a low-wedge cabin fairing into an almost flush deck. Although only a foot shorter than EGREGIOUS, she was actually much smaller. She was also a much better boat, both in design and construction. Olin Stevens is arguably the designer of the century, and RESURGAM's first owner had his own workmen put in a beautiful and functional interior.

Between her purchase in Ipswich, England, in 1983, and her sinking off Florida in 1992, I completed my second, made my third, and began my fourth circumnavigation on her. By chance I closed the circles of circumnavigations II and III in Taiohae Bay, Nuku Hiva, in the Marquesas Islands. Most of the passages during those years I sailed with Jill, who was then my wife.

RESURGAM was a sloop. By 1984 I had come to trust jib-furling gear and had it installed in the British Virgin Islands. From that point, RESURGAM became a three-sail boat: a 135% furling jib, a main, and a cruising spinnaker. Although I carried a few other sails, I never used them.

I still navigated by sextant when I bought RESURGAM; by the time she sank I used GPS.

Self-steering was by Aries windvane, a later model than that used on EGREGIOUS. In nine years it worked perfectly, requiring only an occasional freshwater rinse, lubrication, and the replacement of one bolt. RESURGAM had an inboard diesel, so I also had an autopilot which I sometimes used when under power near shore.

Resurgam is Latin for 'I shall rise again'.

I first came across the word in a biography of Sir Christopher Wren, who reportedly incorporated a piece of rubble inscribed *resurgam* from old St. Paul's into new St. Paul's. In that context it obviously referred both to Christ and to the cathedral.

In 1983, after a year during which a publisher with whom I had a book contract went out of business, my grandmother, who was my only close relative, died, I was imprisoned in Saudi Arabia and later went through a divorce, I named the boat RESURGAM as an affirmation that life would get better. And for a while it did.

---

1 9 8 3

April, bought RESURGAM in Ipswich, England, where I left her
   while sailing CHIDIOCK TICHBORNE II from Egypt to Malta
July, flew to England and sailed RESURGAM to Vilamoura,
   Portugal, where I left her while I flew to Malta and sailed
   CHIDIOCK TICHBORNE II to Vilamoura

1 9 8 4

sailed from Portugal in January and continued westbound
   circumnavigation begun in CHIDIOCK TICHBORNE I and II,
   closing circle in December at Nuku Hiva, Marquesas Islands

1 9 8 5 — 1 9 9 0

made third circumnavigation, also westbound, again completing
   circle at Nuku Hiva, Marquesas Islands

1 9 9 0

continued west across South Pacific to Sydney, Australia

1 9 9 1

October, sailed east from Sydney for New Zealand, via Lord
   Howe Island

1 9 9 2

January 15, sailed from New Zealand for Uruguay via Cape Horn
February 27, rounded Cape Horn
March, arrived Punta del Este, Uruguay
April, sailed Punta del Este to Rio de Janeiro
June, sailed Rio de Janeiro to St. Thomas, U.S. Virgin Islands

July—August, departed St. Thomas for Key West, Florida, collision with ship off Puerto Rico. After repairs in Puerto Rico, arrived Key West

August, sailed Key West to Fort Lauderdale, Florida

August 15, 3:00 a.m. RESURGAM sank approximately ten miles off Fort Lauderdale

August 16, 5:00 a.m., after swimming twenty-six hours, reached anchored fishing vessel off Sebastian Inlet, approximately 125 miles away

12 *Nautical Roulette*

Circumnavigating sailors become spoiled, though they might be surprised to hear so. For most of a trade wind circumnavigation, the wind is fair and there are no major routing decisions. The trades blow from the east, so you sail west. Except during the various hurricane/cyclone seasons, nothing too terrible happens in the trade wind belts, and there is some fine sailing there.

Aboard RESURGAM I could quantify fine sailing: the sloop was making at least six knots more or less toward our destination and the foredeck was dry enough for me to sit there after lunch, lean back against the lifelines, and listen to a couple of cassettes on a Walkman without getting wet, preferably in the shade of the jib. Sounds idyllic, and it was. It even happened. I have been in enough bad weather to savor the good.

Sailors can circumnavigate without leaving the trades with only a few exceptions. One of these is the first leg to get on the merry-go-round. Most sailors live in places with worse climates than they will face in the rest of the world, which is why they often have the worst weather of their entire voyages at the beginning.

You can get around South America to the north while remaining in the trades. You will have to cross the doldrums twice in a circumnavigation. I have crossed them and the Equator ten times, almost always in boats either without an engine or with one that was inoperative, and have never been slowed much. Only twice will most circumnavigating sailors leave the trades, and one of these is optional. From the Pacific islands down to New Zealand can be avoided, but in my judgment shouldn't be. The distance is about eleven hundred miles due south from Fiji to New Zealand's Bay of Islands, and only the last half is unpredictable. But Africa presents greater problems. You will have to leave the trades no matter which way you go around Africa. Having gone both ways, I prefer south. When you approach from Australia and Bali, the wind is usually fair all the way to Mauritius. But from Mauritius to Durban is a sixteen hundred mile passage from the tropics to the Thirties, across the weather patterns. There is no way when you set sail from Mauritius to predict what will be happening when you approach Durban. It is nautical roulette. You spin the wheel and trust yourself and your boat to live with whatever turns up. Even if you have voyaged mostly in the trades, by the time you reach Africa, you are calling yourself a sailor, so it is time to be one.

In 1985 we had two gales between Fiji and New Zealand. In 1987, we had one gale between Mauritius and Durban. That one storm was worse than the other two combined, and the worst natural disaster in the history of South Africa up to that time, with floods causing hundreds of deaths and hundreds of millions of dollars in damage. Except for the cyclone in Tasman, it was also the most severe storm I have been in outside the Southern Ocean.

We first heard of the storm on a BBC radio broadcast while enjoying fine sailing about six hundred miles off the coast. It had taken us a week to cover the first thousand miles from Mauritius. It would take another week to cover the last six hundred. And twenty hours for the last eight miles. The only redeeming feature of that storm was that it blew mostly from the southeast, which enabled us to reach and run ahead of it. Except for the threat of freak waves caused by wind against the Agulhas Current and eventually concern about approaching a lee shore, RESURGAM handled the weather well once we let her broad reach under bare poles.

Before we went to bare poles, however, the sloop took three knockdowns. She went so far over, things came adrift in the cabin that had never done so before. We thought the masthead must have gone in the water. The masthead wind instruments were still in place, the only proof that it had not. We had long since lowered the mainsail, and the jib was furled beyond storm jib to T-shirt size.

So little sail was set that I did not think reducing it would make any difference, but it did. RESURGAM was making six and seven knots and the heeling force caused by those few square feet of sail was just enough to enable the steep waves to throw the sloop onto her beam. As soon as I furled the jib completely, the knockdowns ceased, and we continued on at 5.5 to 6.5 knots with the Aries steering easily. The lesson here may be that when conditions are truly unacceptable, do something even if you don't think it will work.

We entered the storm on a Sunday night. On Monday we began to pick up Capital Radio, a commercial station near Durban, which recited an increasing litany of disaster: floods, landslides, washed-out bridges, rising rivers and deaths. On Tuesday we learned that Durban Harbor was closed to all shipping because of breaking waves.

For us the wind was continuing from the southeast. RESURGAM continued to make one hundred and twenty-five to one hundred and fifty miles a day under bare poles. At this rate we would be on the coast on Thursday with no place to go or hide. For the first time I tried to drag lines to slow a boat down. On RESURGAM, perhaps because the lines were not large enough, this did not work.

On Wednesday morning, when we were only a little more than a hundred miles offshore, I set, also for the first time, a para-anchor. For a few hours this did stop us completely. But setting it was an ordeal under storm conditions, which is the only time you would use it, and, as the manufacturer warns, the line to the anchor is subject to incredible strain and chafe. Despite my eventually getting three layers of chaffing gear in place, the line parted after only a few hours.

The wind was then about fifty to fifty-five knots and the seas about ten to twelve feet. Other sailors who were in that storm described the waves as up to thirty feet. RESURGAM rode to the para-anchor uncomfortably. We were not entirely sorry to hear the twang of the snapping line and feel the sloop's bow fall off downwind. Held by the para-anchor, RESURGAM felt hobbled and trapped; falling free, she came alive. The lesson here may be that it is better to wait and do nothing. Pick one of the above.

The one thing Capital Radio did not give us was a useful weather report. We always waited anxiously for the forecast after the 6:00 p.m. news. Huddled over the radio in a wet, bouncing cabin, night after night we hoped to hear that the storm was at last clearing. Instead we were granted such information as, "Well, the weather tomorrow will be a lot like today. Rain. Rain. And more rain." And the ultimate: "The forecast is so depressing, I'm not even going to read it tonight."

On Wednesday RESURGAM continued onward at six knots under bare poles toward a coast whose only two harbors within three hundred miles, Durban and Richard's Bay, were closed to all shipping. The only yacht that attempted to enter Richard's Bay was wrecked and its crew killed in breakers across the harbor entrance.

The disturbing joker in all this was the Agulhas Current. The Indian Ocean's counterpart to the Gulf Stream, this is a river of warm water flowing south along the east coast of South Africa at three to five knots. Confronted by contrary winds, it can create freak, violent waves. It is also reputed to be strongest near the one hundred fathom curve, which at Durban is ten miles offshore.

Dawn on Thursday at last brought a change. The wind was still blowing at Force 8 and 9, but it had veered to the south. No longer could we sail toward Durban under bare poles. But also no longer was the coast a true lee shore. After a few minutes' hesitation, we unfurled the jib to storm-jib size and continued onward. We were already in the dangerous zone of the current and would cross the one hundred fathom curve during daylight.

Expert advice—if there is such a thing—about freak waves says that they do not occur in less than one hundred fathoms of water. It also claims that, in gales off the east coast of South Africa, the sailor should move as close to shore as possible.

By noon the wind was a solid Force 9 blowing from the south directly against the current. RESURGAM continued to roll onward through the rain. Great storms at sea have no color, but are black and gray and white, constantly shifting. Black waves become white as they break. Gray clouds become black with rain. Much of the time Jill and I observed these changes while standing, clinging to the overhead rails in the cabin, trying to see out the narrow cabin ports.

Early in the afternoon, the radio gave us the good news that Durban Harbor had reopened to shipping. Then the bad news: The first ship to enter the harbor had been thrown by a wave against the breakwater and holed her bow.

RESURGAM's depthsounder usually began to get readings at about 730 feet. At 5:00 p.m. the 700 feet alarm sounded and we knew we were nearing the one hundred fathom curve. The waves were now about fifteen feet high. Standing and staring out, we thought, "She cannot rise to this one. This one is going to break. It has to. It is going to roll her." But they never did. As the last touch of light left the sky, we reached the inside edge of the current, and the waves obediently dropped to six feet. For the first time in several hours, we smiled.

One curious fact is that we were never set south by the Agulhas Current. While in Mauritius I had asked one of South Africa's most experienced racing sailors if, once clear of Madagascar, he would steer for a point well north of Durban or sail the rhumb line. He said the last time he made the passage, he had aimed north, but was headed by a southwest gale as he neared the coast, so this time he would sail the rhumb line. We were glad we followed this advice.

After dark we proceeded with an instrument landing. The depthsounder showed steadily shallower water. The radio direction finder showed a signal from near Durban Harbor at the expected angle. And the SatNav—the less satisfactory predecessor to GPS—got to stay up late. All these indicated that there was a continent ahead. In conjunction, we believed them. But until a little after 9:00 p.m. it was an act of faith in black boxes.

Then, almost simultaneously, we saw lights ahead, the wind and waves decreased further, the SatNav declared that we were eight miles from the harbor entrance, and the shipping forecast on the radio claimed that at last the storm system was on the move. It seemed we had made it.

I decided to sleep for two hours, then sail slowly to be off the breakwater at first light. But something—several things—went wrong. When Jill, who had been standing watch, woke me at midnight, the wind had gone southwest and increased to forty knots. The waves had doubled, and RESURGAM had been pushed far north. The harbor lay directly to windward and RESURGAM, which usually sailed well to windward, seemed reluctant to do anything but point at the nearby shore or head straight back out to sea.

I decided to power. But the Indian Ocean had been hard on the sloop's electrical system. Twice waves had shorted out the ignition switch to the Volvo diesel. In Mauritius I had the switch replaced. As we approached Durban, the new switch also failed and I had to remove the control panel and hotwire the engine.

None of the engine instruments was working either, so I could judge rpm only by sound and had to worry about the alternator and the oil pressure. When the engine sounded about right, our speed was only two to three knots. That should get us to the harbor at dawn, I thought, as I struggled to remain awake for the rest of the night.

A SatNav position at dawn disillusioned us. It claimed we were now eighteen miles from Durban. My curse woke Jill. "This just can't be true," I said. Or words to that effect. "How could we be eight miles off last night, power all night, and be eighteen miles off this morning? We couldn't have been blown that far during the two hours we hove to." But daylight revealed a coastline of low green hills and a mud-colored sea full of bamboo, cane, entire trees, and, although we did not see any, the bodies of hundreds of people. A speck at the far end of those hills, barely visible to windward, was the bluff marking Durban Harbor's entrance.

Unwilling to push harder with the engine without knowing if we were over-reving it, we partially unfurled the jib and headed first in as close to the shore as we dared, and then, tacking to starboard, south. All that day we fought our way to Durban. We passed a dozen ships anchored offshore, obviously the backlog from when the harbor was closed.

By early afternoon we had sailed far enough south so that finally we were able to come about onto port tack and steer for the bluff. When we had to fall off to go under the stern of one of the anchored ships, we ran afoul of a tide that was pouring out of the harbor. We tacked back and forth, making little progress. Sunset was only two hours away, when I said, "We may blow up the engine, but the only way we are going to get in today is to power."

Sitting in the bottom of the cockpit, I again sorted out the various wires and got the engine to turn over. A glance over the side verified that some water was coming from the exhaust. There was not as much as usual. I attributed this to my probably having the engine at lower rpm than usual. By boat speed we were making four knots; by spray coming over the bow we were doing the best possible. The harbor entrance was only two miles ahead. Again it seemed we would soon be in. But it was all too much like the experience I once had with CHIDIOCK TICHBORNE at Tahiti. We no longer cared about hot showers and food. It would be more than enough simply to sit quietly in the cabin tied up securely somewhere and not have to spend another night at sea—this once I would have broken my rule about not entering unfamiliar harbors at night. For that matter, Durban was no longer unfamiliar. We had been looking at it long enough. The problem was getting there.

Both Jill and I were in the cockpit, taking turns steering. "Would you like a can of Coke?" I asked. She nodded her assent, so I climbed down the companionway into a cabin full of smoke and a bilge overflowing with oily water. "Cut the engine," I shouted. "Something is on fire." The combination of water and smoke led us to the culprit, a cracked muffler. I had repaired this with underwater epoxy when I couldn't find the proper replacement in Australia. Certainly the storm had thrown RESURGAM around more than enough to crack it again.

With the engine idling, the wind and tide were rapidly carrying us yet again away from the harbor. We put the bilge pump on automatic and the engine in gear, setting the throttle now not by sound but by volume of smoke billowing from the locker leading to the muffler. The race between wind and tide and setting sun and smoke ended in what I prefer to call a tie. No waves broke as, in a cloud of smoke, we crossed the bar and entered Durban at 6:00 p.m.

As always, the transition was miraculous. One moment we were struggling against the storm as we had been for five days; the next we were in sheltered waters. Within half an hour we were tied to a dock. Within an hour the officials had cleared us and that hot shower and food we had tried to convince ourselves we did not really care about were irresistibly available.

Thin Water

From time to time I see my life as, among other things, a cartoon.

Years ago, while sailing CHIDIOCK TICHBORNE between Singapore and Aden late one afternoon just south of the Persian Gulf, a supertanker steamed up from the south and came to a stop directly in our path. Expecting the ship would move, I did not change course. But the tanker remained persistently in place. CHIDIOCK sailed on for an hour and the ship loomed ever larger. As CHIDIOCK continued to sail and the ship continued to loom, a cartoon appeared in my mind's eye: In the first two frames, CHIDIOCK sails toward the tanker. In the third, the 800-pound sailboat's bow nudges the 500,000-ton supertanker's side. In the fourth, the supertanker rolls over and sinks. In the last, the little yawl sails blithely across a sea from which a few bubbles are rising.

Half a world and more than a circumnavigation later, the cartoons appeared again, twice in one day, when I was caught by a May storm in which the New Jersey coast became a lee shore. For a while it seemed I was going to face the indignity of being shipwrecked right there in Atlantic City in the middle of a podiatrists' convention.

I had left Beaufort, North Carolina, a few days earlier in RESURGAM headed for New York. The wind was from the east, backing slightly and therefore heading us. For a day and a night we crawled north and tried to keep off the shore about ten miles to leeward. There was thick fog, so the existence of the shore was postulated from charts, SatNav positions, and radio direction beacons. It was also cold, with air temperature, water temperature, and wind speed all in the forties.

I was dividing my time between reading, glancing out the companionway at the fog, and checking various electronic displays. The SatNav was giving fixes every hour or so. The radio direction finder showed the Atlantic City beacon to be receding behind us. The depthsounder verified we were staying in sixty feet of water.

One of the adjustments I had to make when sailing the East Coast of the U.S. was to revise my definition of 'deep water'. Being off soundings was a fond but distant memory.

Now, in the fog, my main concern was shipping. We were well inside the main traffic separation lanes to New York, but I worried about smaller coastal vessels and fishing boats. At about 2:00 p.m. I was startled to glance out the cabin port to see what at first I thought was land but which, as I moved to the companionway for a better view, became a tugboat. She was only two hundred yards to leeward or I could not have seen her at all. As I stood there, getting doused by waves and spray, I determined that she was moving about a knot faster than we were on a gradually converging course. Her course was the one I would have liked to be holding myself, parallel to the coast. The question was whether she had a tow and, if she did, whether we would clear it.

During the next fifteen minutes in which the tug and RESURGAM continued to move slowly closer together through their small, intimate world of fog and rain, the answers were gradually revealed to be yes and no. The tug was towing a flat barge piled high with sand and RESURGAM would not clear it.

Waves were smashing into the side of the barge. This close she seemed to be carrying a rapidly eroding beach. And suddenly there flashed the newest cartoon, this one a single frame in which several men stare down from a pier into the vast barge, empty but for one man holding a teaspoon of sand and asking, "Where do you want me to put it?"

I let RESURGAM fall off the wind, swing behind the barge, and gybe. It was so much more pleasant for a moment not to be hard on the wind. I was cold and wet. My fingers were swollen as they had been years before in the Southern Ocean. The prospect of spending the night watching for ships—which I probably would not see anyway until they were upon us—and not making more than twenty miles in twelve hours, all coalesced into an abrupt decision to turn back to Atlantic City, where I could spend a comfortable night anchored off Mr. Trump's marina.

As quickly as this decision came, the tug and barge disappeared. We were alone in the fog, making seven knots under double reefed main and deeply furled jib.

I went below to the chart table. Absecon Inlet at Atlantic City is a straight channel with a minimum of twenty to twenty-five feet of water. A radio beacon at the south side of the entrance should help us find the place in the fog. But the chart did show a bar where the depth might be as low as fifteen feet about half a mile off the mouth of the inlet. The southwest to northeast trend of the coast was decisive. I would not be sailing into a dead-end trap. With the wind slightly north of east, there was an escape route broad reaching to the south without having to come back hard on the wind if something went wrong.

Still, doubts about closing with a lee shore in such limited visibility alternated with doubts about spending the night blindly dodging shipping lanes to one of the busiest ports in the world. The waves were about ten feet high and steep. Surely they would become steeper as we moved in and the water shallowed. It all ended with RESURGAM sailing at seven knots, the waves behind us and the radio beacon ahead. We aren't committed, I told myself. We are just going to take a look. With the very first intimation of danger we will ease off southwest and gain sea room again, even though that means going in the wrong direction.

A replacement for the bolt which had fallen out of the Aries windvane a couple of thousand miles earlier still had not caught up with me, so I was using the electronic Autohelm for self-steering. Ducking back into the cabin from time to time to be certain we were still sailing toward the radio beacon, on deck I stared into the fog, searching for land and watching the depthsounder record ever shallower water. In half an hour it read thirty feet, then returned to forty, and I realized that we had passed over the first of the shoals and were about two miles from the shore.

For ten or fifteen minutes I saw nothing. The depthsounder showed the water to be moving steadily through the twenties. The waves had grown steeper and higher, building to twelve feet. Many of the crests were on the verge of breaking. I was becoming increasingly anxious. What would happen when wave height equaled water depth? Would we go aground in the troughs?

Suddenly something appeared through the fog, rain, and my salt-encrusted eyeglasses: A brown line against the gray sky and sea. There were buildings and a water tank, but I could not see any break in the surf line or any water leading inland.

To get a better view I was standing in the cockpit, hanging onto the lifeline for balance, when the first wave broke over us. My eyes on the shore, I had no warning before RESURGAM went over onto her side. I hung onto the lifeline, half in the sea, the sea half in the cockpit. RESURGAM righted herself and I turned to find myself looking up at the neatly folding top half of another twelve-foot wave. A hard, tumbling, twisting, disorienting blow. RESURGAM was over on her side again; righted herself again. White water poured from her deck, half filling her cockpit, completely filling my foulweather gear.

Fleetingly the day's second cartoon appeared: RESURGAM being carried by a foaming crest right across the beach onto the board-walk, where she comes to rest, undamaged and upright on her fin keel. In red foulweather gear and yellow seaboots, I climb down, nod to the gathering crowd, and disappear into the nearest casino. After the span of time necessary to eat a good steak and salad, enjoy a couple of whiskeys, and visit the roulette wheel, I reappear, walk through the crowd, and climb up the ladder, hundred dollar bills falling negligently from my salt-encrusted parka. The rope ladder is pulled up and sails set. And in the last frame, RESURGAM speeds down the boardwalk on a broad reach.

Back in whiskey- and steak-less reality, I punched a new course in the Autohelm, bringing the sloop's bow back to the wind, cranked in the main and jib sheets, and then took the tiller myself. Sixty feet of water had come to seem like the Marianas Trench.

I hand steered through the next few waves, taking them at a less dangerous angle ahead of the beam. By the time I had a chance to glance back, New Jersey had vanished like a bad dream—something I understand people have been advocating for years.

When we reached thirty feet of water, the sailing settled into the unpleasant but not immediately threatening conditions that had preceded my sighting the tug. I had time to eat a can of tuna and spent the night tacking between the ten and twelve fathom lines. We got nowhere; I saw nothing; eventually I slept a little.

By dawn the wind had died completely, but the fog was still

with us and the waves remained high, materializing suddenly a boat length away. I let them throw us around for an hour and then turned on the engine. We powered and sailed and powered and sailed through shy wind and intermittent fog all day.

RESURGAM was about a mile offshore as we approached Sandy Hook. I could see the outline of something that seemed out of place. It took a moment for me to realize I was looking at the first hill in one thousand miles, rather grandiosely named 'The Highlands of Navesink' on the chart. But then if you are the first hill in so great a distance, you are entitled to an exalted name.

The fog had lifted to perhaps five-mile visibility as we rounded Sandy Hook near sunset. I let go RESURGAM's Bruce anchor in twenty-five feet of brown water and then sat for a few minutes in the cockpit.

I was tired. My neck hurt from being whiplashed by the waves off Atlantic City. The light came on in the nearby lighthouse; a few cars drove along the street running up the spine of Sandy Hook; some ships moved in the shipping lanes a mile north of us. Two fishing trawlers raised anchor and gracefully swung out their booms, before heading into the night, reminding me of the prawn boats I had seen along Australia's deserted northeast coast. On the misty horizon to the west was the vague outline of Staten Island. But, particularly after the storm, everything was quiet. Even without the fog, there would have been no indication that we had just entered one of the world's great ports. This was one of sailing's unique pleasures. Imagine coming to New York and being impressed by the quiet.

Perfection

I finish reading and set the typewritten pages aside with a curious blend of sadness and detachment. The words were written less than a year ago, but on the other side of the world; and so much has happened, so much has changed since then.

I stand and walk through my friends' house. Hemmie is writing a note at the kitchen table, and Bill sits at the computer in his office. I push the sliding glass door to the patio and go outside. The late September New Hampshire air is crisp and clear. The sun warms my skin. Before me unbroken woods, flaming into color, descend a valley, then rise to mountain peaks several miles away. The only sound is the wind in the trees; the wind that has been so much a part of my life that I once wrote that it is as essential as blood.

Although I could not write them now, let the words stand. They were what I thought and felt at a time when Jill and I were happy and had unexpectedly brought RESURGAM to a state of perfection. For me she was the perfect boat. Bill says that this is my most unique achievement. He does not know of any other sailor who thought, even for a moment, that his boat was complete.

This morning while performing the Immelmann turn which permits me to exit from the forward berth without waking Jill, I realized with a start that we have nothing to do today. Rather dangerous thinking a thing like that in the middle of an Immelmann. I almost hurt myself. The deck is painted; the bottom freshly antifouled; the brass polished. Jill has caulked the ports and chainplates and sewn new lee cloths for our sea berths. I have even epoxied the wobbly handle on the tea kettle.

Not until I was standing at the stove—itself polished and with several parts newly replaced—waiting for the coffee water to heat, did it really hit me; and, of course, instinctively, I said, "No. It can't be." But it is. RESURGAM is finished. This is equally odd and unexpected. Not least when one considers that RESURGAM was launched fourteen years ago and has been sailed almost twice around the world since I became her second owner in 1983.

I pushed back the companionway hatch, stepped up, and glanced through the new dodger at the cottages of Russell, New Zealand. Partly it is New Zealand's fault that this has happened. We didn't plan to finish the boat. Really. We were just preparing for a ten thousand mile sail around Cape Horn to Uruguay and Brazil, then somewhere else, and things just got out of hand.

I still don't know where we will go after Brazil, and we are departing in less than three weeks. From previous circumnavigations, charts are aboard that will enable us to continue to Europe or the Caribbean or South Africa. Having been around the Horn before, I know that the Southern Ocean often changes plans. We'll decide in Punta del Este or Rio, assuming we reach them relatively intact.

A month ago, after clearing in at the Bay of Islands, we sailed down to Auckland with a long list of items to be purchased and work to be done on the boat. Two weeks later we sailed away with everything completed on or before time and at less cost than expected. In some ways it was similar to being in Fiji, which Jill considers to be the best place in the world to buy dress fabric. Because she makes most of her own clothes, I can hardly complain, but I did once point out that we were going broke buying bargains.

In New Zealand we have spent more money than we should when I think about it. So I try not to think about it. None of the money was wasted. We are going to do some hard sailing. We have no other serious vices. And, along with a biography of Emile Zola, it was in the way of a fiftieth birthday present for me. For once, however briefly, a sailor should have his boat exactly the way he wants it. And if not at fifty, then when? RESURGAM is. Amazing. I still can't get over it.

The crowning moment came last evening when I tore out, crumpled up, and tossed away the perpetual list of changes, repairs, and needed purchases.

Having disposed of my list, I thought I might have difficulty recalling everything we have accomplished. But I have only to look around. RESURGAM's first owner, an Englishman, would never recognize the boat if he sailed past her, or even if he came aboard.

Fortunately when I bought the sloop in April 1983, the U.S. dollar was strong and she was a bargain, for I have probably come close to doubling her initial price of $36,000 since then. Still she is home and that is inexpensive housing for nearly a decade. Besides she goes to windward better than most apartments.

The very first thing I did to RESURGAM, other than change her name from LADY K on the basis that it is unseemly to sail a boat named after another man's wife, was to paint out the ugly gray fake teak deck. I don't even like real teak decks, which are hot underfoot in the tropics, require maintenance and eventual replacement, and put weight too high; but I accept that some boats don't look right without them. I can't imagine why anyone would want to have fake teak.

The next changes were to add a manual windlass, a second anchor and chain, and a self-steering vane. I did this after my first sail in RESURGAM, from Ipswich to Brighton.

The windlass was the Hyspeed model manufactured by Simpson Lawrence, who should be ashamed of themselves. I did not know then that this unit is justifiably notorious for a drive train of bicycle chain. RESURGAM is low profile, low windage, and only displaces 11,000 pounds. She is as easy a boat on an anchor as any out being seriously sailed. Nevertheless the bicycle chain was more often broken than usable between 1983 and last year when I replaced it in Australia with another manual windlass, this one made by Maxwell. The Simpson Lawrence Hyspeed might be quite appropriate for raising an anchor used by a bicycle.

The windvane is an Aries, which has steered 95% of the time since I installed it. A bolt fell out a couple of years ago in the Old Bahama Channel, and it wasn't until I reached Boston that I was in one place long enough for the replacement part to catch up with me. In the interval, an Autohelm 2000 steered. Otherwise the Aries has required only the occasional fresh water rinse and WD40.

I sailed RESURGAM from England to Portugal and then across the Atlantic to the British Virgin Islands before doing much else to her. In the Caribbean I had jib-furling gear installed and upgraded the electronics with the then state-of-the-art Brookes & Gatehouse 190 system. I also replaced the conventional spinnaker with a cruising chute in a squeezer bag.

The furling gear is probably the most important change I've made. Although I had the luff tapes on the storm jib and working jib converted, I have never used them, and did the entire next circumnavigation with the 135% furling genoa. RESURGAM has become a three-sail boat: 135% furling genoa, main, and cruising spinnaker, with the first two needing to be replaced each circumnavigation. At the moment I have it worked out so I get a new main in New Zealand and a new jib on the other side of the world.

For the next several years we made many minor improvements as we sailed around the world, adding an electric bilge pump, replacing cabin lamps and stereo speakers, adding a CD player, reworking the saltwater pump and tap in the galley five times before they finally came right.

We acquired a SatNav in Fiji and a new propane galley stove in New Zealand in 1985. We had the hull painted burgundy in Australia in 1986, and bought new cushion covers in South Africa in 1987.

There were many other changes too, such as buying a couple of solar panels, installing a solid boom vang, which enabled me to eliminate the topping lift, always an annoyance at sea; and removing and disposing of the reel halyard winch, which I have not liked since one on EGREGIOUS released prematurely and caused a winch handle to smash me in the mouth; and leading the main halyard back to the cockpit.

While the boat was merely one of the first owner's toys, she has been my only home, so I have finished off some of the interior woodwork he left undone, adding a second bookshelf forward, a door on the hanging locker, a rack for CD's, a piece of trim around the opening where the mast passes through the overhead.

I also removed the refrigerator. Americans can't live without their fridges, I keep being told. And most U.S. cruising boats do have them. But then so do most U.K. cruising boats, and French and Kiwis. Why the first owner had one on a boat he used only for the rare daysail in the North Sea during the impostor that masquerades as summer in those waters, I do not know. In any event, it drew too much power and I gave it away to an impecunious Spaniard. The switch marked Refrigerator on RESURGAM's electrical panel now controls the depthsounder.

Damage—the headstay parting off Cape Hatteras and the Volvo diesel dying in Panama being the major incidents—has played a part in RESURGAM's evolution.

We will never know for certain whether the Volvo could have been saved. We do know that, despite Jill's fluency in Spanish, we did not want the hassles of attempting to have it repaired in Panama. So we jury rigged a rented fifteen-horsepower outboard to the Aries support brackets to transit the canal, and proceeded under sail to Australia, where quotes for rebuilding the Volvo came to as much as a new Yanmar. We went new and have regretted the decision only during the installation, an ordeal enhanced by the mechanic not reading that the Yanmar shaft turns clockwise viewed from the stern, and the Volvo doesn't. The sea trial was terminated prematurely when I pushed the lever forward to leave our mooring and we went backwards. About $900 for a new Gori folding propeller—changing to a folding prop from a fixed blade was another change I made back in 1984 after RESURGAM's first Atlantic crossing—and all has gone well.

At a total cost of $7,000 U.S., about half for installation, the new diesel was by far the biggest single expense in RESURGAM's career. Given our average of one hundred and twenty engine hours a year, I am counting on the Yanmar to outlast me.

We also installed a fireplace in Sydney. This required major surgery in the form of removal of a locker on the main bulkhead, shortening an overhead grabrail, rewiring the music system, and cutting a hole in the deck, which is always traumatic.

We have yet to light a fire under sail, but the fireplace was invaluable while living aboard in Sydney Harbor during the winter.

The other major additions were sensibly deferred until our arrival in Auckland, where we took delivery of a new mainsail, my first with full battens; new halyards; a dodger; and a GPS unit.

Our last mainsail was made here and had lasted a circumnavigation plus two additional crossings of the Tasman. The price difference between a new sail from Hood's loft in Sydney and their loft in Auckland was 30% in favor of the Kiwis, and less than half U.S. prices. I had some reluctance about full battens. So far the sail has behaved perfectly, but so far has only been three hundred miles and I reserve judgment for thirty thousand more.

When I removed the reel halyard winch, I went from an all-wire halyard to a rope/wire splice on the main. When the headstay came down, I went to an all-rope jib halyard. Now, coinciding with the arrival of the new main, an Auckland chandlery had a special of 40% off all rope, which drove me into a feeding frenzy: a new Spectra main halyard, a new jib halyard, a new mainsheet, a new jib-furling line, and a new Spectra outhaul. These permitted an old jib halyard to replace a spinnaker halyard, which was then cut into new reef lines and traveler control lines, led to new clam cleats, which seem to be holding, where a succession of cam cleats over the years did not.

RESURGAM had a full width dodger when I bought her. On the passage from Brighton to Portugal I found it inconvenient and never used it again, finally disposing of it in Antigua. Having run the Aries control lines to within hands' reach of the companionway, we do not spend very much time on deck in bad weather, so a dodger's protection did not seem important. I found that I could furl the jib and reach most of the lines more easily from the companionway without a dodger. Additionally, I just don't like the way they look. Arnold Schwarzenegger once said, "The human body should be a work of art, and most people look like junk." A boat should be a thing of beauty, and most people junk them up. So RESURGAM will never have a windmill to generate electricity, rusty bicycles, assorted jerry cans on deck, or even a barbecue hanging over the stern. That she now has a dodger just the width of the companionway is a compromise I have only reluctantly accepted to solve the problem of taking water below in heavy weather.

I take pride in being good with a sextant, probably because the skill was self-taught and hard earned. Pride cannot withstand technology, and when the price of SatNavs dropped to $1,200 U.S. in 1985, I installed one. I confess that I have seldom used a sextant since.

In a vague way I thought that when GPS approached twenty-four hour a day world wide coverage and prices dropped below $2,000 U.S., I would buy one; 1991 proved to be the year. In Auckland the nearest chandlery had a new Sony unit on display for $1,800 U.S. I held out long enough to telephone the U.K. and the U.S. and establish that the unit was not yet available in either place, before I took one home.

GPS is literally, almost disconcertingly, a revelation. I don't plan to throw away my sextant, but I know it won't see the sun except in an emergency or on fine days when I might take a sight or two to prove I still can. I expect that some boats are going to be lost because people trust GPS positions beyond the accuracy of charts, or have no one aboard who can navigate when the electronics fail. I have already met a man who abandoned his yacht at sea and permitted himself and crew to be taken aboard a passing freighter solely because his SatNav broke a few years ago on a passage from New Zealand to Fiji. What was most peculiar was that he didn't even seem embarrassed.

The last time I went to the Horn, in sleet and snow, I got no sextant sights for the five days prior to my mid-December rounding, and, to be safe, I headed further south, sighting the Diego Ramirez Islands, but never Horn Island itself. This time I want to see the rock. I have already entered the waypoint in the Sony.

Stasis is not possible nor even desirable to achieve. The laws of entropy apply to boats. I'm sure something will break soon, and the tiller can always use another coat of varnish. But that is merely maintenance. RESURGAM really is finished. There is no other equipment I want to buy; no other changes I want to make; and I don't ever want another boat.

The problem of what to do with the rest of the morning remains. Perhaps we'll just have to raise anchor, go over to the Custom's Dock, and leave.

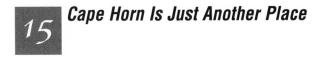

15 Cape Horn Is Just Another Place

When the wind backed east, we were not worried. After all we were eleven days out of New Zealand, bound, as our clearance papers proclaimed with some flair, for "Uruguay via Cape Horn," and at 42°S and 160°W well within the province of the celebrated westerlies of the Roaring Forties. Thus far on the passage no wind had lasted more than twelve hours without shifting at least 90°. The relevant square of the pilot chart categorically denied the possibility of wind between north-northeast and south-southwest. This aberration would soon end. In the meantime, with the easterly at eighteen knots, the sailing was not too bad and the late January temperature not too cold, although enough spray began coming over the bow to drive us from the cockpit.

We were ahead of our expected rate of progress since leaving Whangarei on the afternoon tide of January 15, 1992. As I returned our shower key, the woman in the harbormaster's office had asked where we were going. I told her and added, "It is only the first mile I am worried about."

Whangarei is, as I had been advised by other sailors, the most convenient port on the North Island. If you don't draw much more than our 6'3", you can enter the town basin, some twelve miles up river from Bream Head, and be in the heart of the central shopping district. But you must do so on the top half of the tide, with the last mile being a long S not shown on the chart. The channel is marked by posts, but on our way in, the depthsounder had shown us to have only inches of clearance in one or two spots. I had taken the gamble and removed our anchor from the bow for the long open ocean passage. I could only too vividly imagine the hassle of digging it out of the cockpit locker along with the dinghy and the oars, inflating the dinghy, kedging off, being stuck, being frustrated, wasting time.

In the event that did not happen. When we were safely in thirty feet of water, we unfurled the jib, let the autopilot steer, and broke out a couple of cans of cold beer bought at the last minute with our refunded key deposit. Despite our lack of refrigeration, cold beer did not figure to be a novelty on this voyage.

A dying tropical cyclone, downgraded as it weakened in colder waters, pushed us away from land, and did not catch us until long after New Zealand's rocky East Cape vanished in the rain. As it did, we realized that we were sailing East Cape to East Cape. Uruguay's Punta del Este lay six thousand miles almost due east.

For Resurgam the depression provided gale force winds from the west and seas rising to twelve to fifteen feet, a taste of what I had come to know in the Southern Ocean on my first circumnavigation. But as I said, only too prophetically, to Jill, "A gale from astern is better than twenty knots from ahead."

As Resurgam moved easily ahead of the cresting waves under only a scrap of jib, I thought how different this was from my Cape Horn passage sixteen years earlier. In 1975-76 I was alone on Egregious, a similar though slightly larger boat, on which, following bad advice, I usually kept some of the mainsail set and had no jib-furling gear. As a result, Egregious was often overcanvassed; and I spent a lot of wet, uncomfortable time on the foredeck. Now, if I was older, I was also, in this at least, wiser, and kept Resurgam moving without being as hard on her or on myself as before.

While in Whangarei we had gone to the only movie theater to see City Slickers in which middle-aged men talk about what were the best and worst days of their lives. For me the day that came immediately to mind, or rather the moment, was that afternoon of December 11, 1975, when after five days of sleet and snow in which I could get no sextant sights, I managed a snap fix of the sun through clouds which indicated that the Diego Ramirez Islands should be ahead, and I knew that, even if the mast came down, on the following day I would pass Cape Horn. Although I was later to set world records and this was only an American first, still because I had been dreaming and struggling toward it for so long and because it was my first real achievement, it was the one I recalled most fondly; unlike love, where first love cannot compare with last.

The differences between 1992 and 1975 were many. I was with Jill and not alone. Resurgam had an engine, electrical system, a jib-furling gear, solar panels, a dodger. I was navigating by turning on a GPS unit smaller than a Walkman, which did not exist in 1975, rather than using a sextant. The two most fundamental differences however were that at age fifty I was on my fourth circumnavigation where at age thirty-four the world was new to me and Cape Horn a frontier; and that I had come to expect that RESURGAM would not break, where EGREGIOUS almost always did.

I thought of music as the east wind not only persisted, but strengthened to twenty-five knots. We had been looking forward to this long passage, to settling into the great rhythms of the Southern Ocean. From experience I knew that the concept of giant waves rolling right around the world in those landless waters is a delusion. But we were looking forward to broad reaching in strong winds, sliding down good size waves, RESURGAM's bow wave curling above the deck, slashing through the sea, reveling in the power and majesty of the Southern Ocean. We had last made such a passage crossing the Indian Ocean four or five years earlier from Bali to Mauritius, though then in tropical latitudes and in warmer, reinforced trade winds.

Such rhythms are Beethoven and Brahms. Now as we shortened sail and pounded to windward, the rhythms were short, staccato, erratic, jerky, uncomfortable. Instead of a romantic symphony, we got heavy metal. Literally a couple of nights when blocks broke on the mainsheet. Digging through my spares locker, I found two forgotten blocks which were exactly what I had unsuccessfully tried to buy in New Zealand. It was not until after I had replaced the second block—the swivels failed on both—that I realized that, with the slack mainsheet, the new fully battened mainsail had feathered peacefully into the wind, where our old conventional main would have been flogging itself to death.

The east wind became a nightmare.

RESURGAM sailed well to windward, too well at times for her own good. On a long passage—and our first waypoint was still four thousand miles away—it is better to go fast than point high; but as the wind remained doggedly at 115° and we sailed 45° to 50° off to the south-southeast, the seas steepened. RESURGAM began to leap off waves with shattering regularity.

The wind increased to thirty, then thirty-five knots. We furled the jib more deeply. When we clicked the Aries off to a broad reach while we tied another slab reef into the main, we had a momentary vision of an unattainable paradise. Our speed went over seven; the motion was easy. This was the wind angle we had a right to expect. This was the way the travel agent had promised it would be. The problem was that we were heading southwest and did not wish to visit Antarctica. Jill tailed the mainsheet as I winched it in. Then, with simultaneous sighs, we both ducked through the companionway. I clicked the Aries lines to bring RESURGAM's reluctant bow back to the war.

A grid compass positioned on the aft end of the saloon table could be seen from our sea bunks at night. Night after night we awoke, and hour after hour, night after night, always we were disheartened to find the wind unchanged, the luminescent lubber line far outside the luminescent V set for the desired course.

For two days the wind was Force 7, gusting Force 8; but the barometer was high and steady and the sky cloudy. In increasing gloom, mental and meteorological, we sailed down to 45°S, where the wind continued to head us beyond endurance. I was willing to sail south to get east, but not west of south. At 45°S, we tacked to starboard, and gradually the wind headed us again. The new oversized, overstrong lee cloths Jill had made for this passage were well tested as we jolted on, day's runs deteriorating.

The wind decreased to twenty-five knots, but remained east. Even the trade winds aren't that steady. I studied the pilot chart in disgust. This simply could not be happening.

A week passed. An entire week of easterlies in the Roaring Forties. It was unheard of. I had expected us to average five knots getting clear of New Zealand, then six knots to Cape Horn, and five knots again from the Horn to Uruguay. Our first week we made good an average of 5.7 knots. The second week our average fell to 4.9. The third 4.0. Despite having seventy gallons of water aboard, we cut our consumption. Only one cup of coffee in the morning and no tea at night. Holding cups was too difficult anyway.

Secured in our berths we read and forgot the words a moment later. Despite the motion, Jill managed to bake every second or third day the whole grain muffins, fortified with powdered milk, muesli, and raisins, that were our staff of life, and to heat water for freeze dried meals at night. Sequential thought became impossible. Life was spasmodic and episodic. The simplest tasks became ordeals, demanding complete attention while maintaining balance. Every moment night and day the force of gravity was an intrusive reality rather than an abstract law.

In the southern hemisphere an east wind could be created by a high passing south of us or a low passing north, neither of which was normal. The barometer remained high and steady. Could there really be a big high precisely keeping pace with us? Or was this a consequence of an El Niño year? In New Zealand we had heard experts proclaim that an El Niño would cause New Zealand to have a wetter summer than usual, unless it caused the summer to be drier. No one even wanted to speculate what an El Niño would do to the wind in the Southern Ocean .

Day after day we pounded east, gradually being forced from 45°S back up to 42°S, where we tacked again. Finally back at 45°S and at 129°W, the barometer dipped, rain began, and the wind backed to due south.

The following morning saw some blue sky and a continuation of the wind's backing. "Well, it has finally happened," we told one another as we emerged to sit in the cockpit for the first time in two weeks. "We have found the westerlies." RESURGAM was making an easy 6.8 knots toward the Horn. After all the beating, she hardly seemed to be moving. The only worry was that the wind was continuing to back.

Two days later it steadied due east again. Hope of fine sailing and a fast passage had long since died. This was not epic; this was trench warfare, footslogging drudgery, plodding through knee-deep mud, step by step, wave by wave. It could not be happening, but it was. And for seven more days RESURGAM fought against a perverse east wind. Though we eased her way as much as possible, we could not help but wonder how much she could take. Twenty to thirty waves a minute stressing the hull, the rig, the furling gear.

The temperature dropped as we moved further south, but it was not until our last week before the Horn, with the wind west at last, that we were able to use our fireplace. On a mooring in Sydney, it had helped us through an Australian winter, but we had not yet tried to use it under sail. At 50°S the cabin temperature was 40-45°F. We were wearing several layers of clothing and sleeping comfortably under two sleeping bags each, which we used as lap robes during the day. With the waves finally from astern, I opened a bag of charcoal and carefully made a fire. The wind built to gale force, only our second true gale since leaving New Zealand, though three times the east wind had gusted Force 8 from a solid Force 7. On deck the temperature dropped to just above freezing, with the wind chill much lower. Inside we grinned at one another as the cabin temperature rose to 70°F. Never had a gale been so enjoyable, and at last we were having a thousand mile week. The best sailing is also the easiest.

February 27, the day of the Horn, dawned hard and spectacularly clear. Although the GPS pinpointed us still thirty miles west, Horn Island's pyramid face was visible at the end of a chain of purple mountainous islands. I had not seen Horn Island when I rounded fifty miles south in 1975, and wanted to pass as close as possible.

The wind died in mid-morning. We turned on the engine to power rather than be thrown around by eight-foot swells caused by the shallow continental shelf. In 1975 a Force 12 wind created twenty- to thirty-foot breaking seas on that shelf. My body still remembered the tremendous power of those waves.

As we neared Horn Island at noon, clouds spilled over the now gray mountains to the north and cold rain began to fall. Ominously the wind came from the land, backed north-northeast and increased to twenty-two knots. Horn Island disappeared along with our hopes of building a fire that afternoon. Going to windward in more than twenty knots, too much water came over RESURGAM's deck to open the chimney. It doesn't really matter too much, we thought, for we had planned to pass east of Staten Island and perhaps even the Falklands; but now, after beating most of the five thousand miles east to the Horn, our first afternoon trying to go the fifteen hundred miles north to Uruguay found us closehauled. That evening I did manage to play the Bach fugues I had listened to in 1975; this time on compact disc.

Staten Island, whose jagged peaks are somewhat reminiscent of Moorea if its climate is not, lay in bright sunshine just north of us the following afternoon. We sat on deck, watching albatrosses fly around us. There was so little wind that they could not glide, but were reduced to flapping their wings. Life was tough all the way around. When the wind returned at sunset, it was from the north.

Each of the next three afternoons found us becalmed. Each night found us closehauled against north wind. The headwinds lasted for ten days, from 56°S to 41°S. East wind when we wanted to go east, twenty-four of the first thirty-four days of the passage; and north when we wanted to go north, for twelve of the last fourteen days to Punta del Este. In all we were hard on the wind for thirty-seven of fifty-eight days at sea.

Those first afternoons were not unpleasant. Each day birds hunted around us, and on the third, the albatrosses found the work too hard and began to settle on the water, dropping and folding their wings, as we dropped and furled RESURGAM's sails. More and more birds landed, more than we had ever seen or even expected were in our vicinity, until finally a silent RESURGAM sat on a mirror-smooth sea surrounded by several hundred of mostly silent birds. The birds looked at us. We looked at the birds. The birds yawned. Well, it was that kind of a passage. Being honorary albatrosses is an interesting way to spend a slow afternoon. Not until a light breeze returned near sunset did our flock disperse.

That night we saw a loom of lights to the northeast. It appeared to be the light of a substantial city, but the chart did not show anything on that bearing. On Falklands AM radio the next morning Jill heard that a Japanese fisherman who became ill had been airlifted from a large Japanese fishing fleet. For the following two nights we did see boats in the distance, but avoided the floating city. Those days we noticed a great many dead birds in the water: penguins; what appeared to be swifts; albatrosses; cormorants.

At 42°S, the wind still ahead of us, a cloak of thick fog of several days' duration lifted, and we were able to shed the remnants of our woolly cocoons and expose our pasty bodies to the sun. Perhaps because of the fireplace or perhaps because we basically stayed dry, even off the Horn the cold had not been as severe as I remembered. Now we were sunbathing in the Forties. The sea was a gently undulating meadow. Even if we were not moving very fast, making only three to four knots closehauled against five to six knots of wind, we had only a little over three hundred miles to go.

The wind increased and boxed the compass the final twenty-four hours of the voyage, so that appropriately we found ourselves closehauled against a twenty-five knot northeasterly as we crossed the wide mouth of the River Plate. Landfall should have come at dawn. The GPS put us only ten miles offshore, yet nothing was visible in thick coastal fog. Trusting machines more than I care to—another said we were in sixty-five feet of water—we pounded on. Nothing but jagged waves, more of the dragon's teeth we had known seemingly forever. New Zealand was a fading memory. Finally I caught a glimpse of something. "Is there a hill near the coast?" I asked Jill, who had visited Punta del Este a decade earlier. "Not that I recall, " she replied. The outline was lost, then reappeared and firmed. What I had mistaken for a hill was a cluster of high rise apartment buildings. We lowered the mainsail, furled the jib, and powered slowly forward while I shackled the Bruce anchor to the chain.

Fifty-eight days and almost seven thousand miles. It had been slow; hard on the boat and hard on us; but we had not known any really severe weather or big seas. Except for the two broken mainsheet blocks, a flashlight lost overboard, and a minor tear in the spinnaker, we had not sustained any damage. Jill had become a Cape Horner and could now keep one seaboot on the table whenever we toasted the Queen.

I realized that I had thought that this passage would be a completion for me. And it was, though not the completion I sought. I had sailed toward the greatest moment of my life, the time when I had the most hope my life would have meaning, and of course it was not the same. For sixteen years, from the moment I first passed it, I had known that I would return to Cape Horn. Now I had, and I felt an unexpected sense of loss. I needed new capes. In a few months one would appear. I would have more than just a sense of loss, I would have the reality.

Though it had not been an easy passage, it had not been epic either. Some years Cape Horn is just another place.

"This is it, Jill," I said, but it wasn't. RESURGAM was destined to survive for another month. When I spoke I expected her to sink within seconds.

We were about ninety miles northwest of Puerto Rico, 3:30 a.m. on a clear full moon night, broadreaching before twenty knots of wind under furling jib at seven knots. I had checked less than ten minutes earlier and seen nothing. The bright moonlight and perfect visibility may even have contributed to the collision. Running lights, ours and the ship's, would have shown up better on a darker night. Of course, radar would have helped; but even after sailing recently on two boats equipped with radar, I don't regret not having it. The current drain is too great for my kind of boat, and radar-equipped ships still run into one another. The ship that ran into us was new and modern and surely had radar, and I know that RESURGAM gave good returns.

I had glanced about less than ten minutes earlier. It was a big ship, several hundred feet long, and I had not seen it. RESURGAM's masthead tricolor was lit. Her jib was a great silver triangle. Still, assuming we were closing at a combined speed of twenty knots, together we would have covered more than three miles in ten minutes. The Aries was steering RESURGAM. Who knows who or what was steering the ship. On the bridge, the helmsman looks down, daydreams, looks away, sips a cup of coffee, gets involved in a conversation with the watch officer, if there is one, and for the last half mile or so a sailboat is hidden beneath the bow.

We had deliberately sailed far north of our rhumb line course from St. Thomas to Key West via the Old Bahama Channel in order to be away from shipping, and had not seen a single ship all that day or night. It is difficult to figure out where this one was headed so far away from the usual shipping lanes. Her course was east; ours west. Perhaps she too had gone north so her crew could sleep.

A grating, twanging sound. Metal to metal. Harsh. A giant file rasps the strings of a giant guitar. I look out the port and say, "This is it, Jill."

She sits up and stares at a rushing wall of metal. Although I believe it is painted red, in the moonlight it appears darker, the color of dried blood. "It's a ship," she says.

Our voices are normal, flat, declarative. We freeze for a moment, expecting to see the ocean pour into the cabin. The terrible sound of grinding metal continues for a few seconds, then ceases. Inexplicably water does not appear. "Try to reach them on the VHF," I say and jump for the companionway.

The ship's squared-off stern towers above me. Perhaps I could read the name and port, but at that moment I am not interested. I still expect that RESURGAM will sink. My impressions are of a big, modern, container carrier. Most definitely she is not a Caribbean tramp. I turn my eyes from the ship to RESURGAM.

The ship has passed to windward. We are still in her lee, gliding slowly. Our freeboard does not yet seem to be reduced, but we must be sinking. As I open the cockpit locker to get the dinghy and jerry cans of water, I hear Jill's voice through the companionway. "This is the sloop RESURGAM calling the ship that was just involved in a collision with a sailboat ninety miles north of Puerto Rico. Come in, please. Do you hear me? Come in, please."

The radio is a handheld unit with a ten mile range. With a sense of relief, I see the ship slow and turn beam on to us half a mile astern. If we have five minutes, we can abandon ship, prepared well enough to reach land by ourselves. If we have only one minute, we probably can't. But with the ship returning, we will survive. Then I realize that Jill is still in the cabin. With the inflatable half out of the locker I stop and call down, "Is there any water coming in?"

"No."

How can that be? I wonder. I duck my head through the companionway. The cabin is startlingly normal. For the first time it occurs to me that we might not be sinking, and if somehow we aren't, then damage control is more important than preparing to abandon ship.

I move forward along the lifelines, lean out, and stare down at RESURGAM's hull. The starboard upper shroud is slack in my hand. Above me the broken starboard spreader clatters against the mast.

RESURGAM has a single spreader rig, and the mast is flexing grotesquely, bending through more than forty degrees of arc. Finding no visible evidence of hull damage, although there are areas of the hull I cannot see, I run back to the cockpit and pull on the Aries control lines to gybe the sloop and bring the wind to the port side of the boat.

As the jib comes across, the mast bows almost to a right angle, snaps back, and holds. I trim the jib sheet and run forward to bring the spare jib and spinnaker halyards and topping lift to the toerail to act as shrouds. For a moment I stand beside the mast and stare up into the night. Although we are now sailing with the wind slightly ahead of the beam into five-foot waves, the mast is almost steady and almost straight. I return to the cockpit and furl the jib to half size.

I pause. Not much time has passed since that first squeal of metal against metal. Two minutes; perhaps three. Jill is still futilely calling the ship.

"Shall I send out a Mayday?" she asks.

"No. If we're not sinking, we can reach land by ourselves."

"Why doesn't he answer? Do you think there's something wrong with our radio?"

"I don't know." As we later established, there wasn't.

Even at a distance, the silent ship seems big. Slowly her stern turns toward us, then she gathers speed and rapidly powers away to the east. Beyond doubt the collision has not gone unnoticed.

"May an albatross hang around your neck," Jill calls over the radio from the companionway. We both go below deck. The cabin still seems normal, and considering what has just happened, normalcy and relative silence are eerie.

I push the Mark button on the GPS and plot the position. The concern is not survival now, but, first, how to reach land without losing the mast and, second, to find a place where repairs can be made. The Dominican Republic is downwind, but I know nothing of it and have no detailed charts. We do have a seven-year-old cruising guide to Puerto Rico, although we had only sailed to San Juan to get visas and a cruising permit for Venezuela in 1984. San Juan, I think, is too far to windward, but a port called Mayaguez halfway down the west coast of the island looks possible.

Jill checks the bilge. Over her shoulder I see that it is essentially dry. She stands and says, "It just does not seem possible."

"No. I don't understand it either. To be hit by a ship that big and not be holed; not, as far as I can see, even to have a scratch on the hull. Why don't you start the engine, while I put Mayaguez in the GPS?"

By the time I had finished at the chart table, a dawn more welcome than most was lightening the sky, and we were able to make a more thorough search for damage.

On my first solo circumnavigation, I was capsized three times, mast in the water, in the Southern Ocean, and in RESURGAM we had taken a few knockdowns. You don't ever really know what happens at such moments. You just try to piece them together later. In this instance, all we would ever find was damage aloft.

The starboard spreader, still attached to the upper shroud at its outboard end, had snapped off near the mast. Jill subdued it with one of the other halyards and its own flag halyard. A single strand of the wire shroud was broken. The masthead wind instruments were hanging down, as was the masthead light, which was still working. There was a shallow dent on the forward side of the mast about three feet below the tabernacle, a kink in the jib-furling foil at the same level, and an adjacent one-inch hole in the jib, all of which were surrounded by smears of red paint. The hole where the bolt securing the upper shroud tangs pass through the mast was bigger.

RESURGAM's rig was all well inboard. She had the tumblehome common to designs of the 1970's and her chainplates were several inches inside the toerail. All of which leads to the conclusion that RESURGAM passed almost the full length of the ship before rolling her rig to windward and catching something extending from the hull near the stern, or perhaps being turned toward the stern by the Aries when it was blanketed by the ship. I would like to have been a sea bird, soaring high above us in the moonlight. The burgundy sailboat and the great red ship approaching one another across silvery, moonlit waves. The sailboat's course varying by ten or fifteen degrees as she slid down crests. Within a hundred yards, she may well have been directly in the ship's path; she may have been pushed aside only at the last second by the bow wave. The two vessels must have been only inches apart for half a minute, perhaps more, before we knew.

"You were lucky," some people said when we reached land; and some misguided souls even called me lucky a month later. To the extent that character is destiny, and that is by no means as certain as American myth would have us believe, I am neither lucky nor unlucky. Spend years at sea, instead of ashore talking about going to sea, and something will go wrong, sooner or later, and perhaps both. Something, many things, will also go right. In either case, the experience will be intense, and whether pleasure outweighs pain, or joy redeems sorrow, is a matter of individual and capricious judgment. At times life seems too short; and at other times much too long.

With a deeply furled jib and the engine at moderate rpm's, we motorsailed southeast, hoping to reach port before dark. Some of the seas were hitting us forward of the beam and causing the mast to sway ominously. I cut back the engine a little and let out a little more jib. I also moved our new Spectra main halyard to the starboard toerail as a running backstay and tightened it with a winch. This was the strongest, lowest stretch line on the boat. When it was in place, the mast seemed solid.

In late afternoon, land became visible for a few minutes before being obscured by the usual thunderstorm over the inland mountains. Dark clouds and heavy rain passed ahead of us, and it was not until just before sunset that we found smooth water in the lee of the land. We were still ten miles from Mayaguez. Under the circumstances and with the help of a rough sketch in the outdated cruising guide, we broke our rule of not entering port after dark. Of course the buoys marking the entrance through the reef had been changed and at least one of them was unlit, but the approach was straightforward and we certainly did not want to spend the night wallowing around outside. At 10:00 p.m. the anchor went down well away from the bright lights of the commercial wharf.

"Well, we made it," Jill said. And for the moment it seemed we had.

Ahead of us lay another long day and night of powering along the south coast in a futile attempt to return to St. Thomas or at least reach the east side of Puerto Rico, where the bigger boat yards are located, all dismally to windward. I don't know that the mast would have survived. Each time we came off a wave, the mast flexed. I counted an average of twenty-five waves a minute. Times sixty meant one thousand five hundred an hour. Times twenty-four meant St. Thomas was thirty-six thousand waves away.

I was fatalistic. The mast would either stay up or it wouldn't. If it did, we would do one thing; if it didn't, we would do another. But the engine decided otherwise by sputtering, probably from a dirty fuel filter, twenty miles east of Ponce, Puerto Rico's second largest city. The cruising guide said that there was a yacht club at Ponce, but was vague about facilities. For us the place had the incomparable virtue of being to leeward, although the last quarter mile of our approach would have to be made with the jury rigging to windward. This could not be allowed to matter. We had no choice. RESURGAM was not going any further.

The engine seemed grateful. Instead of laboring east at three knots into a short, nasty chop, which had not diminished at night as we had hoped, we made an easy six knots back to Ponce, and anchored off the yacht club just before nightfall.

"Well," Jill said, "we made it." And once again, it seemed we had.

That was Saturday night. The collision had taken place Wednesday. Although the yacht club does not have a working repair yard, with the help of some members, RESURGAM's mast was pulled and re-welded, and the shroud replaced.

The repairs themselves took very little time, but there were inevitable delays waiting for tides that would enable us to get RESURGAM to the dock, and for parts to be sent from San Juan to repair the forklift that was used to pull and re-step the mast.

We were both anxious to be on our way again. This was July. The hurricane season had begun, and we had sailed more than thirteen thousand miles since leaving New Zealand for Cape Horn in January. We were weary, mentally and physically, and needed to come to rest.

On the second Sunday after we reached Ponce, the mast was re-stepped, and the next day we sailed for Key West. Thirteen days had passed since the collision, almost half a lunar cycle.

The worst is behind us, we thought, as we happily headed west across the Mona Channel on a dark new moon night. I had felt unusual pressure all that year. Move on, move on. Get the miles done. I had chaffed at each delay: almost forty days beating to windward during the long passage around the Horn, including that improbable three weeks of easterlies in the Roaring Forties; an extra week in Uruguay, waiting for lost mail; several weeks in Rio, so Jill could have her surgery. I could not know, but perhaps I sensed, that we were rushing to destruction. The next full moon would be RESURGAM's last.

Swimming

I pulled the plug at midnight.

Specifically I removed the transducer for the boat speed indicator which left a 1 1/4-inch diameter hole through the hull just forward of the mast. A column of water shot through this hole almost two feet into the air and began to fill the cabin. I straightened up and watched the water for a moment before nodding my head once, a single dip of my chin, then turned and climbed into the cockpit.

Ten or twelve miles to the west, the lights of Fort Lauderdale reflected across low waves. It was a pleasant, starry August night; the wind light and warm. I sat quietly as the sloop continued to sail east, away from the land.

After a little more than an hour, I leaned forward and looked through the companionway hatch. Several inches of water covered the teak and holly cabin sole and splashed onto the lower berths whenever the boat rolled. The level was disappointing. I climbed back down and opened the locker in the galley where Jill kept the pans. Warm sea water swirled around my ankles as I pulled the pans from the shelves and lifted the bottom of the locker, exposing the engine's water intake. From the tool locker above the galley I took a screwdriver and stooped to loosen the hose clamp around the seacock. Even without the clamp, the hose remained stuck to the seacock. I had to pry it off with the screwdriver. Another column of water, 1 1/2 inches in diameter, began to enter the cabin.

By habit I started to return the screwdriver to its proper place. Jill, when she first began to live and sail with me, had protested that I was too particular. In time she came to understand that it is necessary for everything on a boat to have its place where, even in bad weather, it can be found quickly. But no longer. I dropped the screwdriver where I stood, heard the splash, and climbed back up on deck.

With the increased flow, the sloop began to sink more quickly, but still another hour passed before I felt the change: a lurching out of synchronization with the waves, a heaviness, a slowing of motion, as though she were tiring.

There was no sound from the cabin now that the intakes were below the rising water, and I peered through the hatch again to be certain. The level was much higher, covering the lower berths. Cushions were floating, papers, the tea kettle we had bought a few months earlier in Uruguay. Out of curiosity, I turned the ignition key for the diesel. Nothing. The batteries and electrical system were below water. The engine was almost brand new. It had less than two hundred hours on it. I had thought when we re-powered in Australia that this engine should last the rest of my life, and so it would. I gave a small smile.

Behind me the shore lights had fallen below the horizon. Only the loom was visible, a glow stretching fifty miles from Miami to Palm Beach.

I sat calmly, a tall, lean figure, expressionless once the smile faded.

At 3:00 a.m. on Saturday morning, the sloop's bow dipped beneath a wave as it had millions of times in the nine years during which I had owned her. But this one was different. Although only a foot high, it was RESURGAM's last. Her bow did not break through, doggedly or triumphantly, as it had in every latitude from beyond 50°N to beyond 50°S, in near survival storms to gentle trade winds, from the English Channel to the great Southern capes. This wave ran up the deck to the mast, before hesitating for a moment, as if surprised by its temerity and success.

The bow sank lower beneath the water; the stern rose several feet into the air. In the steeply inclined cockpit, I pulled myself to my feet, stood up, and glanced about the deck one last time. I had made voyages other people had thought were impossible, but which I had believed I could accomplish. Now as I stepped over the lifelines into the warm ocean to die, I was about to do something even I considered impossible.

RESURGAM's stern loomed above me, echoing scenes from newsreels of ships sinking in World War II. No home port was shown. My home waters, I had written, were the world.

The rudder and propeller were exposed. I noticed a gooseneck barnacle on the strut that I had missed when I snorkeled to clean the bottom a week earlier in Key West, after the completion of the passage from Puerto Rico, in a year that had seen us cover fourteen thousand miles in seven months. I thought: I miss New Zealand. I miss the Southern Hemisphere. The North Atlantic has always been my least favorite ocean. That barnacle made a mistake. It will not survive the depths toward which RESURGAM is headed. A thousand feet of water beneath us. I made a mistake too. I never should have returned. All the decisions seemed reasonable when they were made. Yet they brought me here.

RESURGAM's stern rose higher, then slid down, and disappeared. A few ripples. A few bubbles. No suction. Some loose objects, which had been possessions, but were now strange and foreign in the black water, drifted around me. I swam a few strokes to get clear of them. Everything I owned, except for the T-shirt and shorts I was wearing, and the elephant skin billfold I had put in my pocket, thinking that the plastic credit cards might be the only way for anyone to identify the body, in the unlikely event it was discovered, was gone. Everything I loved lost within a few hours.

I pulled the eyeglasses from my head and let them drop from my fingers. I could not see through the wet lenses, and I would not need them any more. The shore lights became diffused fuzzy spheres. With small movements of my hands I turned away and faced out to sea. I leaned back in the shimmering water, stared up at the full moon, and let my mind wander.

I had sailed so much that I was always meeting myself, crossing tracks on charts from different years. Because I did not consider that I had spent much time in the Caribbean, I had been surprised when I pulled out the Caribbean chart on the passage a few months earlier from Rio de Janeiro to St. Thomas to see how many small penciled x's marked noon positions from past voyages. One line entered from the east from Portugal to Antigua in 1984; another from Portugal to the British Virgin Islands a circumnavigation later in 1989; then a line from Antigua to the British Virgin Islands in 1984; and one from the British Virgin Islands north of Cuba to Key West in 1989. All these I had made alone.

There was the track from Roadtown in the British Virgin Islands south to Venezuela, where I had sailed with Jill when she joined me in 1984; and along the coast, then out to the offshore Venezuelan islands, to Bonaire and Curaçao and Panama, where she unexpectedly left for the first time; followed by my track alone disappearing off to the west to the Marquesas and Tahiti. A line ran south from Key West through the Yucatán Straits to Panama and west to Tahiti that Jill and I had made in 1990, when we were reconciled after a fourteen month separation.

With the increase in the price of charts, I kept them and marked RESURGAM's position with ever lighter and smaller x's. Several hundred charts were aboard RESURGAM at the end. When Jill had unexpectedly returned in 1989 and we decided to sail to Australia, we had to buy only one new chart and that was the first one around the west end of Cuba.

There were so many places, so many images. I had been in almost constant motion for two decades. When I was falsely jailed as a spy in Saudi Arabia in 1982, the police required me to account for my past travels. I discovered that I had not been in one country for more than two months during the preceding four years. Memories clicked through my mind like slides on a projector: Portugal where Jill and I first met on Christmas Day in 1983 and spent our third wedding anniversary in 1988; South Africa; Sydney, Australia, the single place where we had stayed the longest; Lord Howe Island; Bali; Europe; South America; Namibia; New Zealand. The images crowded in too fast, blurred, stopped. My mind became a blank screen.

I was calm. I was Socrates after drinking the hemlock, waiting for the numbness to move upward from my feet, asking, "Why should I fear death? For when I am, death is not. And when death is, I am not."

Courage did not enter into this. I had lived a certain way, and it had brought me here. "Live passionately, even if it kills you, for something is going to kill you anyway," I had written; and now it would. "Intensity, not duration," I had written; but against all odds I had lasted fifty years.

A little wave, the first of many, too many, splashed into my face. Sputtering I let my legs drop and came upright in the water. I pictured RESURGAM sailing through the depths below me, her new mainsail still set. I wondered how long it would take her to reach the ocean floor. I had wanted her to be my last boat and Jill to be my last woman. Now both were. But I had not expected it to be so soon.

That mainsail was less than a year old. It would easily have carried me through the completion of another circumnavigation. The engine, less than two years old. The dodger and GPS and windlass were new in New Zealand the preceding December. The bilge pump had been purchased only a few weeks earlier in Puerto Rico.

I let myself turn slowly until I faced the distant shore lights. I was a good swimmer, but I had never tried to swim so far. It was at least ten miles, and I had never swum a mile at a time. There is nothing for me there, I thought. I deliberately turned and swam a few strokes further out to sea, but then I stopped and leaned back and floated. I thought of RESURGAM again. What will it be like down there? I speculated idly about how far my body would sink, and how long it would be before I weakened and drowned. Staying afloat was so easy.

Another little wave lapped over my face. I came upright. Treading water was more comfortable than floating. I looked at my watch and was surprised to discover that it was already 4:00 a.m. I had been in the water an hour, which seemed only a few minutes. Less than a week earlier, Jill and I were snorkeling near Key West and I had gotten out of the water, slightly chilled, after only forty-five minutes. I undid the watch strap and let the Casio I wore at sea fall away. In the moonlight, the water was extraordinarily clear, and the watch remained visible for several seconds. My hands, moving slowly near my waist, were pale.

I didn't know what I expected, perhaps weakening, loss of consciousness, oblivion; but nothing was happening. I was in England in 1983 when Rob James, one of the sailors I respected, drowned off Salcombe Harbor. But that was February. Hypothermia. You would not last long there. Or off the Horn. I thought of the modern Greek novelist and poet, Nikos Kazantzakis, who imagined Ulysses leaping into the Southern Ocean after walking the length of Africa, striking out for the South Pole. I had always rather expected that I would die in the Southern Ocean. "The ocean waits to measure or to slay me. The ocean waits. And I will sail." I had written. And I had sailed and was still here.

This was taking too long. I had possessed everything I wanted materially: the boat; the books; the music; and a few luxuries: in port we ate off Wedgwood and drank Laphroaig Scotch from crystal. I had the boat exactly the way I wanted it. I had the woman I wanted. "It is the end of an era," I had said to Jill as we approached the entrance to Fort Lauderdale only an unbelievable three days earlier. I had meant that the epic phase of my life was over. The plan had been to earn enough in two to four years by lecturing and writing to enable us to return permanently to the South Pacific and Australia. I was fifty. I had done enough. Loved enough women. Sailed enough. Set world records. Done things no one had ever done. Written things which ought to be remembered, but wouldn't be. Returned to Cape Horn and found it unchallenging. Without taking a breath, I lowered my head beneath the sea and swam down.

Only ten or fifteen feet beneath the surface I ran out of air. Instinct, what I call the animal, took over. The mind can say, "You are in a hopeless situation. I do not fear death, only the suffering along the way." But the animal always wants to live, and my animal is strong. It had kept me alive for five months in a damaged boat in the Southern Ocean during my first circumnavigation, bailing seven tons of water every twenty-four hours. It had kept me alive for twenty-five thousand miles in an open boat. It had kept me alive while drifting three hundred miles in an inflatable in the South Pacific, until I reached land unassisted in what is now Vanuatu. Some people said my open boat voyage expressed a death wish. They did not consider that my first circumnavigation, in which I stopped only twice and set American and world records, was for me a baseline. I sailed the open boat because I wanted to do something even more difficult. The panicked animal struggled back to the surface.

Gasping, sputtering, I deliberately slowed my legs and arms. A wave curled over my head. I coughed water. I was getting tired of these waves. They were a bit higher now, though still only one to two feet. The sky was lightening to the east. I turned. Either because they were lost in the oncoming dawn or because I was being carried further offshore, the shore lights were no longer visible. I let myself rotate slowly. In every direction was only the ocean. I stopped myself facing east, and calm again, quietly, dispassionately, observed what I expected to be my last dawn.

I treaded water and floated. An hour or two passed. Perhaps more. I continued to be amazed at how easy it was to keep afloat.

I had been swimming for at least five or six hours, but felt completely relaxed.

I thought of the pioneer French aviator, Saint-Exupéry, writing about his attempt to walk away from a crash in the Sahara. Dying is simple, a natural act, Saint-Exupéry said, as he struggled not to die. He survived the crash, only to die flying in World War II. I wondered what Saint-Exupéry thought in his last seconds, if he had time to think at all. Dying might be simple. Drowning might be a sailor's death. But the animal wasn't having any.

Low mist was turning into fog. For the first time, I shivered. Perhaps this was the beginning of hypothermia. I knew that heat is lost by movement. I was not moving very much. Slow strokes with my hands; an occasional slow kick with my legs. I was seeking neither life nor death. I was simply waiting.

Something, a darkness in the fog, caught my eye. As I watched, it became a small fishing boat. Instinctively my spirits soared. I heard the low throbbing diesel. It would pass close. Not more than twenty or thirty yards away. The engine became louder. I was wearing a yellow T-shirt. I pulled it over my head and tried to wave it in the air, but the shirt was sodden and heavy and stuck to my hand.

When the boat was close, I yelled, "Help!" once. The boat puttered steadily onward. I watched it fade into the fog and disappear. "All right, don't help," I said aloud in a normal conversational tone, struggled back into the T-shirt and turned back toward where a bright spot in the fog indicated the sun and east.

My instinctive reaction to the fishing boat came as a surprise. But there was nothing for me ashore. Everything really was gone. And death is not optional. If not now in the next few hours, then sometime in the next ten or twenty years, probably from heart disease or cancer, more painfully and with less dignity. "That is the trick: to give up a few good years to death before it is too late," I had written in a poem about the death by cancer almost twenty years earlier of the man I thought of as my grandfather. Recalling the words calmed me. I was glad the fishing boat was gone, glad to be alone again. Of the six or seven years I had spent at sea, three or four of them had been alone.

While I slowly treaded water, my movements mechanical, my mind wandering, the fog dispersed. I became aware of the sun heating my face. The sky was blue and clear. I turned toward the west. No land was visible; but even without my glasses I could make out the fuzzy outline of a ship heading north several miles inshore of me. The Gulf Stream would have carried me a few miles north and perhaps a bit east. Land must be more than fifteen miles away by now.

An isolated image flicked though my mind of us having lunch in Rio on the terrace of the restaurant at the top of Corcovado, just below the statue of Christ, while the city appeared and disappeared through the clouds below and humming birds sipped from wild flowers beside our table. I could feel the sun burning my face. No need to worry about skin cancer any more, I thought; but I pulled the back of my T-shirt over my head as a kind of cowl. Evaporation from the damp cloth was soothing.

The sun was almost directly overhead. I had been in the water for nine hours, and was only a little tired. The wind had increased to ten knots. The seas were still low, but dotted with scattered whitecaps. More and more of them splashed into my face. I was not hungry, but thirst was becoming a torment, as it had been when I drifted in the inflatable for two weeks in the Pacific. I felt something brush my leg, then a tentative nip. My leg kicked out automatically. I looked down and saw several small silver dollar size fish scurrying away. "Not yet," I told them. And then, having started, I continued aloud, "How the hell long is this going to take?" The words provided an impetus, and the animal ran with it. Before I knew what I was doing, I had turned and started swimming west.

I stopped. "What are you doing?" I asked myself. "There really is nothing for you there. RESURGAM, Jill, everything, really is gone." The truth was undeniable. The response came not from reason, but from instinct, from thirst, from the saltwater rawness of my face and mouth. I did not think I could reach shore, but I could no longer endure waiting for the sea to take me.

I swam the crawl for a minute or two, before turning to sidestroke, then backstroke, then crawl again. It felt good to swim. After that first instinctive burst, I swam smoothly. My muscles enjoyed the movement. The last time I had swum much had been almost two years earlier in the fifty-meter pool in Suva, Fiji, where I usually did sixteen laps. And now survival was at least thirty times further away, plus a current carrying me north or northeast, while the coast of Florida falls away to the west. It did not matter. "I might not need to reach land," I thought. "I might be seen by a ship. Besides I said I need goals, and now I again have one."

Swimming helped divert my mind from my thirst, but my body remembered. It was as though that earlier thirst when I was adrift in the Pacific was indelibly imprinted in each dying cell.

Pausing every once in a while to float and rest for a few minutes, I swam, chasing the sun west through the afternoon. The wind increased a few more knots, but remained moderate. The waves pushed me; but more of them crested and filled my mouth, which was becoming a raw wound. Breathing was easier on my side, so gradually I found myself swimming sidestroke more than the other strokes combined.

Sometime in mid-afternoon I saw a sail to the south. I stopped and treaded water, hope rising. At first the sail seemed to be heading for me; but as it came closer, I saw that it would pass half a mile or so to the east. I watched silently as a small ketch motorsailed north. I thought I saw someone in the cockpit, but without my glasses and with my eyes raw, I was not certain. I felt a sense of loss when the sail disappeared.

This was the longest rest I had taken since noon, and for the first time I realized that I was tiring. I had been in the water about twelve hours. I had not eaten for almost twenty, or had a drink since before midnight. I was surprised that I still had to pause to urinate occasionally. I did not have much fat to convert into energy. A cramp seized my stomach. I reached down and pressed my hands against my abdomen until the pain eased. It was more hunger than a muscle spasm. A growl from the animal: "Feed me!"

My hands felt strange. I looked down and noticed that half a dozen little fish were hovering around me. As I watched, one of them tentatively approached and bit my khaki shorts, which the fish apparently did not find to its taste. The shorts were chaffing my thighs, as the T-shirt was my arms. I thought about discarding them, but decided they might keep in some heat if I lasted until night.

I raised my hands above the water. They looked like something from a horror movie. The skin was not just puckered, but seemed to have come loose from the muscles. As tentative as the fish, I touched the back of my left hand with the fingers of my right, half afraid the skin would peel away. For the first time I thought of blood and sharks. The skin moved peculiarly, but remained in place. Fear gave the impetus I needed to resume swimming.

Gratefully I observed a line of clouds move in from the ocean and block the sun. Heavy rain began to fall behind me. I stopped and waited, hoping for a drink of fresh water, but the shower passed to the south. When I resumed swimming, I discovered that the sun was completely obscured and I was confused. The wind had increased to eighteen or twenty knots and the waves were higher and steeper. In quick succession three waves broke over me, leaving me coughing and gasping for breath. The waves dictated my course. Despite a probable wind shift with the clouds, I had no choice but to swim before them.

The waves seemed to be helping me. I thought of body surfing off San Diego and Bali. A few years earlier I had been caught by a rip-tide off Bali. People ashore, including Jill, had watched helplessly as I was carried toward Java, but eventually I reached the beach. Now I did not swim hard. I knew I wasn't getting anywhere. More and more waves crashed over my face. Each was a knife cutting my eyes and mouth. I tried to keep my eyes closed, but found that I changed direction almost immediately. And I had to keep my mouth open to breathe. Gargle twenty thousand times with salt water.

"Ninety-eight. Ninety-nine. One hundred," I counted strokes to myself, just as years earlier when EGREGIOUS capsized in a cyclone in the Tasman I had counted buckets full of water. Without thought, without any attempt to reason why, without considering hope or hopelessness, I continued swimming.

The clouds and wind lasted until nightfall. The sun shone long enough at sunset for me to discover that I was swimming more north-west than west. I made a course correction and slowly continued.

I knew I was weakening. I was swimming only twenty strokes sidestroke, ten back, then five crawl. My right elbow hurt, and I did not have much power in any stroke. The moon would not be up for an hour or two. I stopped and waited for some stars to appear so I could determine west. In the increasing darkness I noticed the lights of two ships, one heading south, one north. It took a while before my tired mind realized that they were both a mile outside of me. *Outside.* During the limited visibility in the rain, which never quite fell on me, I had crossed the shipping lane. Momentary elation collapsed when I turned and saw the loom of lights from the shore. Only the loom. Experience said that I was still at least ten miles offshore. The goal for the night could only be to try to turn the loom of lights into specific lights. And to last until dawn.

The night blurred and my mind wandered, pausing at my first night in New Zealand. When was it? I was irritated that I could not subtract two numbers. Fifteen years ago? No. Sixteen.

The water in the bilge was preternaturally still. It was still coming in, but now that EGREGIOUS was tied to King's Wharf in Auckland, it was not leaping and splashing about and it was not coming in very quickly.

I had made the initial transition to land after five months alone at sea with ease that afternoon, swarming up the pilings, standing on land with no sensation that it was moving under me, talking to people. I had bathed in salt water before entering the harbor and must not have looked too bad. People expressed surprise that I had been out so long. They assumed that I had just come overnight from the Bay of Islands.

But now, when I could at last sleep an entire night through, I didn't. I bailed the bilge, knowing that it would not fill again until after midnight, lay down and fell asleep, only to awaken thirty minutes later. For five months I had not slept through a night, and for the past three of those months, I had awakened to bail every half hour. Through habit I lifted the cover and glanced in the bilge. There wasn't even enough water to think about.

I stood in the companionway and watched traffic moving on Customs Street and the lights of the high rise buildings. It was all quite amazing after seeing nothing but ocean for so long. Restlessly I wandered about the cabin, took a book and tried to read but soon put it aside. I tried to go back to sleep and failed. I got up, put on my clothes, and went ashore.

I had not exchanged money that afternoon. Probably I could have done so that evening at one of the hotels, but I didn't think of it, and for that matter I didn't really want to buy anything. Some part of me was curious, some part starved for new sights, new sounds, new sensations.

I was a complete stranger to the shore and the country. I looked at people almost as an alien species.

I experienced everything through a veil of exhaustion. Corners of buildings, stoplights, window displays, other pedestrians, all blurred. And as I walked up Queen Street, my legs quickly gave out. I stopped in front of a takeaway place, called Uncle's, offering the novelty of American hot dogs. It seemed an appropriate spot to turn around.

I was waiting at a stoplight halfway back down the hill, when a woman came up beside me. Through the city smells, damp pavement, car exhausts, her perfume reached me.

The light changed, but I just stood and watched her cross the street.

The cold of the sea, the warmth of a woman. It had been a long time.

I remembered my first glimpse of Suzanne's legs. Her husband brought her with him to see EGREGIOUS in the boat yard and to invite me to dinner. She was wearing a rust colored skirt and a white blouse and sandals. I was working on the hull when they arrived unexpectedly on Sunday afternoon, and I held the ladder for them to climb up and see EGREGIOUS's interior. Her body moved up the ladder only a few inches from my face. Instinctively my eyes followed her. She had nice legs, good ankles. I found myself staring up at her bare thighs, and, not wanting to desire someone I could not have, deliberately looked away.

Two days later, when her husband was at work, she stopped by the boat yard alone. Three weeks later, EGREGIOUS repaired and back in the water, I rowed Suzanne out to the mooring and we made love for the first time.

New Zealand was still Suzanne to me when I sailed there nine years later with Jill, but this last time, it was not. My memories of Suzanne were more than a decade old. No emotion clung to places

I had been with her. It was as though it had never happened. And Jill and I had been particularly happy. That was still this year, I thought, as I swam ever more slowly.

I was in Paris with Jill. On the first fine day of spring, we left our hotel near the Louvre and walked through the Tuileries.

We passed the circular fountain where seven years earlier I had sat one afternoon, watching children sail toy boats. The children pushed the boats away from one side of the stone fountain and then ran, laughing and shouting, to where they thought the boats would touch. Often the slight breeze backed sails and caused a change of course. And there was always the falling water in the center as a permanent squall. I was alone at the time. It was the year between Suzanne and Jill. As I watched the children, I expected that some of them must dream of real voyages, and I wondered what would happen to those dreams.

Near dusk a woman in a burgundy coat came and took the last two of the children, a boy and a girl, by the hands, and they walked together in the lamplight toward the river. She was a very pretty woman, with a sweep of raven black hair, high cheekbones and long legs. I envied the man she was going home to.

Jill and I walked along the Seine to Notre Dame. It was a Sunday and, although mass was being said when we arrived, spectators were still permitted to enter the cathedral. We stood at the back and for the first time saw the church in use, full of people and voices filling the vault with hymns, brilliant colors as the sun blazed through stained glass, the vivid vestments of the numerous priests, one of whom was swinging a censer, warding off evil spirits with smoke in a gesture of ancient superstition.

We sat outside the church beneath cherry trees in bloom, beside flying buttresses and gargoyles, before crossing to the left bank. From the bridge we saw that the ledge below us was filled with pale Parisians in bathing suits, sunning wintry bodies and picnicking beside the dark dirty river, as though at the seashore.

We caught a cab to Napoleon's Tomb. Jill had never seen this one, although we both remembered his first tomb, an unmarked slab hidden in an out-of-the-way spot in a grove of trees down a hillside on St. Helena, where we had stopped on the passage from

Namibia to Europe. There never had been an inscription on that grave because the British and French could not agree on whether to include the title 'Emperor'. When a generation after his death, the former enemies had become allies, his body was moved from the lonely island in the South Atlantic to Paris, where the French built him this grandiose monument.

One of the quiet pleasures of sailing the world is to bring parts of it together: to be able to contrast Napoleon's first grave with his second, and his second with those of Wellington and Nelson in the crypt of St. Paul's in London. The French built more lavishly for their failed emperor than the British did for the victors.

Leaving the tomb, we turned toward the Eiffel Tower and re-crossed the river to find a crowd at the Trocadéro: street musicians, singers, dancers, African men selling windup paper birds that soared in brief bright flight, families out for a Sunday stroll. We stopped and watched a slalom course roller skaters had made with tin cans. Many of the skaters were talented, changing directions at each pair of cans, zigzagging down the paved slope, some doing so backwards. Paris is usually a cold city, but people were remarkably good natured that fine day.

We were hungry and headed to the Champs-Elysées, where we sat in a restaurant and drank a bottle of wine and ate salmon, which was the culinary fad in Paris in 1990 as coq au vin had been in 1983. I actually wanted coq au vin now, but did not see it on a single menu.

We had finished the salmon and decided to order another bottle of Chablis, when from the avenue came loud music. Everyone stopped and several of the patrons rushed outside. A sound truck appeared followed by an open convertible, carrying a young man, who was smiling and waving as people cheered. In a moment the small caravan had passed; the music and cheers receded in the distance toward the Place de la Concorde.

"What was that all about?" Jill said.

"I cannot remember the man's name. We saw his arrival on television the other night after he had just completed the fastest solo circumnavigation."

It had once been my record, but I had not held it for many years.

The waiter brought the bottle of wine.

We rowed ashore to a patch of sand and brush, frequented by frigate birds and boobies, and walked out onto the reef. At Suvarow, one of the few deserted islands in the South Pacific with a usable anchorage, the reef is more volcanic than coral. Those parts washed by the tides have been smoothed through the ages, but near the shore the lava spikes remain almost as jagged as when they first exploded into air. The black reef becomes salmon pink as it is uncovered by the outgoing tide. Brightly colored fish are often trapped in pools of water held by fissures in the lava, trying to hide from soaring birds until they are released by the returning ocean.

I rose from studying a tide pool and turned to see Jill standing with her back to me, looking out at the sea. I felt as though we were on the edge of the world, a primitive, simple world of great beauty in which there were no other people. A vast blue sky and sea, a white turmoil of waves breaking on the outer edge of the reef a few steps away, just beyond which the reef fell off to a hundred fathoms. The lush green vegetation on the islets; a narrow band of white sand; black lava; salmon pink lava; fish; scuttling crabs; the bright sun and the shadows of circling birds; the elegant curves of Jill's naked body. It was a perfect, timeless moment, a rare moment when I felt at peace, a moment I knew even as it was happening that I would remember as long as I lived.

We walked along the promenade in Montevideo.

In a park in front of an apartment building in the old part of town, we saw a goat kneeling to eat grass. A boy turned the corner from one narrow alleyway, riding a fine gray horse. Fishermen perched on the seawall, dangling hopeful lines in the choppy water.

We passed two couples, sitting on benches partially sheltered by the seawall. The couples were only a few steps apart but oblivious to one another. The first couple were young lovers. The second, dressed all in black, were a middle-aged man and an old woman. The woman, whom we assumed to be his mother, was quietly crying. They seemed just to have come from a funeral. Both couples were the same: a man with his arms around a woman, whose face was buried against his chest: the embraces of love and death identical.

Jill and I walked back up the hill into the center of the city where, at a cafe beside the inevitable Plaza Independencia, we shared a bottle of wine in the evening dusk and watched pigeons settle on the statue of Artiga, Uruguay's George Washington.

We were high on a hillside at the north end of Lord Howe Island in the Tasman, four hundred miles northeast of Sydney. We were both naked, both on our knees, I behind her, looking from the upturned soles of her bare feet, to where I was moving in and out of her, my hands gripping the curve of her hips, along the indentation of her spine, the finely defined muscles in her shoulders, tendons taut in her neck, her full breasts dangling, moving with my thrusts, nipples brushing blades of high grass, her face hidden by long blond hair, to where RESURGAM swung on a mooring in the lagoon far below. From that elevation, giant Norfolk pines bordering the lagoon appeared tiny. At the other end of the island, five miles distant, two shear sided mountains rose thousands of feet directly from the sea.

And all these memories will soon be lost, I thought, as I swam ever more slowly.

The overcast sky partially cleared and the moon came out. Despite improved visibility, I found that I increasingly lost my sense of direction and was swimming the wrong way. Only pain was clear and sharp. My eyes, my mouth, my throat, thirst, were intolerable. For a while I felt a painful urge to urinate, but could not. There was no more fluid in my body. My right elbow, bending with each sidestroke, was becoming excruciating and useless. I simply stopped and hung almost motionless in the water more and more.

Two or three times I started to shiver uncontrollably. The Gulf Stream was warm, but it was not body temperature, and I thought each time that this was the end. But each time inexplicably the shivering stopped. Two or three times I was brought up short by swimming into jelly fish. The stings were unpleasant, but not serious. Two or three times my body was wracked with dry retching. There was nothing in my stomach to come up. Two or three times I actually fell asleep for a few seconds, but awoke when my head fell below the surface and I breathed in water. Only a flick of the wrist was enough to keep me afloat.

I made two discoveries. First, that Saint-Exupéry was wrong: dying is neither natural nor simple; and that the weaker and more exhausted I became, the stronger became my will to live. I was "not going gently into this good night." If for the first nine hours, I had been Socrates, now, as I weakened, I became Dylan Thomas.

By about 1:00 a.m., judging by the moon, I knew that I would never reach land. The lights were still only a loom, a glow to the south, then darkness, and two other patches of light further north. I began to hallucinate, while aware that I was doing so. A particular cloud, illuminated by the moon, turned into a filigree of lace each time I looked at it, starting at the bottom and working upward. I rather enjoyed watching the process. And I thought I saw a sailboat, a large sloop, motionless, sails down, unlit, seemingly at anchor. While I was certain about the cloud, I was unsure of the sailboat, and spent some time treading water, studying the image. There really seemed to be straight lines of the rigging and the mast that just could not appear naturally. Sometimes when I looked it was there, and sometimes not. I resumed swimming.

On my right side, facing south, I saw the loom of lights concentrate into specific pinpoints that seemed to be running lights. I dismissed these too as hallucinations; but they persisted and came closer until my mind finally accepted that they really were the lights of two fishing vessels. About half a mile away, they stopped. I continued swimming, slowly, painfully, favoring my right arm, for a few more minutes, then I stopped too.

I hung in the water and considered the fishing boats. One of them remained stationary, while the lights of the other described a long oval in the darkness. Of course I did not know how long they would remain, but I knew beyond doubt that I could not reach the shore. It was not really a gamble to turn south instead of west.

I swam harder than I had since nightfall, trying to ignore the pain in my elbow; but it was like trying to walk on a broken foot. I kept myself from looking at the running lights as long as possible. When I did finally pause to rest, one set was far out to sea, but the other was definitely closer.

I resumed swimming, trying to maintain a sustainable pace. When adrift in the South Pacific, I had been surprised that after two weeks of near starvation and only six sips of water a day, I had enough strength left to row the final four or five miles to land. But that had been a decade earlier. I was fifty years old now and surviving on no sips of water for more than twenty-four hours and no food for forty hours.

I prevented myself from stopping to rest by trying to remember when I last had a drink.

I thought I recalled drinking a can of Coke Friday evening. This was now sometime around 2:00 a.m. Sunday. I thought of Jill, and wondered where she was at that moment. We had separated almost the moment RESURGAM reached Fort Lauderdale. And then I thought about what would have been the last piece of music I would have played before RESURGAM sank. I could not decide from a short list of Bach's unfinished Art of the Fugue; Beethoven's last string quartets; Satie's Gymnopédies.

When I simply could not take another stroke, I stopped, looked up, and saw that the fishing boat was only a hundred yards away. There was no point in saving anything. I took a couple of deep breaths and set out again.

I had not gone more than twenty yards when I had to stop. My body simply had no more strength. When I looked, the fishing boat seemed no closer. I could see the boat's details, the deckhouse windows, the booms. I yelled, "Help!" as loudly as I could. The effort hurt my throat. The sound seemed to fill the night. But there was no reaction from the boat.

I lowered my head and swam, desperately trying to close the gap. But this time when I looked, the lights seemed further away. I swam again. Each time covering less distance before having to stop. Twenty yards. Fifteen. Ten. Yet each time the fishing boat was no closer. Finally, in despair I understood that it was powering slowly away from me. "Don't go," I shouted. But the gap steadily increased. "I am dead," I said unnecessarily.

The effort to reach the fishing boat had exhausted me. I could not swim, but lay back in the dark water, keeping myself afloat with sporadic hand movements. I watched the clouds turn to lace. I began to shiver. I stopped shivering. I became aware again of the torment of my eyes and mouth and throat, and of thirst. This is unendurable, I thought. Unendurable. Part of me would have welcomed oblivion, but it did not come. And gradually, as I floated, I regained some strength.

I came upright in the water. Dawn should only be two or three hours away. I could last that long. And perhaps in daylight another boat would come along. Life had become simple again. Just do one more thing. Bail when EGREGIOUS's hull was cracked. Row when I went over the reef after CHIDIOCK TICHBORNE capsized in the Pacific. Now, swim until dawn.

Floating and swimming a few strokes, then floating, mostly floating, I tried to move west. I began to see the sailboat again. "I don't believe in you," I thought. But I found myself stopping and staring. I really did think I could see the hull and the straight lines of the rigging and mast. I looked away and then back. It was all still there. I still did not believe in the sailboat; but it was not far out of my way, so I swam slowly toward it, breaststroke now, my least effective stroke, but one which enabled me to keep my eyes on the boat and caused the least pain in my elbow.

The sloop remained in place. "I don't believe in you," I kept telling myself; but part of me was beginning to. Then, off to my left, I noticed a light. I turned. My vision, blurred by exhaustion and salt water was suspect, but there seemed to be a white light, an anchor light. I turned my head back to the sailboat. It was still there. Then toward the light. It was still there too. I did not know what to believe, what was real, if anything. Somehow the anchor light made more sense. Giving the sailboat a final glance, I started toward the light.

I did not hurry. My goal was to survive until dawn. I had to swim somewhere, so it might as well be toward the light. I did not have the strength to do more than inch my way. Whenever I looked, the light was closer, but I did not feel the elation I had when approaching the fishing boat an hour or two earlier.

What seemed to be a long time passed. Not until I was close enough to see the hull in detail was I convinced that there really was a boat. It was a small commercial fishing vessel about forty feet long, anchored in the middle of nowhere. There was no sign of activity. No lights except the anchor light. No sound of an engine. This was all very strange and made me suspicious that I was hallucinating. The only way to find out was to swim over and knock on the hull. But as I watched in horror the boat began to power away from me. "Help!" I yelled. "Heeelllppp! Don't go!" The gap between us continued to widen. "Help!" I yelled again. And from the darkness a sleepy voice answered.

"Is there someone there?"

"Over here. In the water. Fifty yards off your port quarter. Don't go!"

"Where? Keep shouting," a second voice called.

"To port. Astern. Don't go."

Deck lights came on. Then a handheld spotlight flicked across the low waves.

"Further out. No, to your left." And the beam found me.

"Where's your boat?"

"It sank yesterday off Fort Lauderdale."

"Fort Lauderdale?" The voice sounded confused.

"Just don't go. I'll swim to you. Just don't go."

The pain was all still there, but I covered the final yards without stopping. The hull rose sheer above me.

The engine was turning over. A voice shouted over it, "Come around to the stern."

"The prop?"

"It's in neutral."

I swam along the starboard side of the vessel and came to the stern. Two young men were leaning over and staring at me. Water from the cooling system and exhaust smoke were bubbling out. "Put your foot on that step and try to reach up."

"I don't have much strength in my legs," I said. My foot slipped, found the step again, and I pushed myself high enough for hands to reach me. I did not think: I will live. I thought: at last I will get a drink of water.

EPILOGUE

1993 -
THE HAWKE OF TUONELA

She waited for me that winter in the snow, not far away, less than one hundred miles to the west. I often looked out the windows of my friends' home and watched the dim changing light on the snow-covered White Mountains, but I cannot say that I dreamed of her. My thoughts were of the past; and the future was the next hour or at most the next day.

When I left New Hampshire, I went more than a thousand miles south, as far south as I could, and sat on the beach in Key West and stared at the sea and my memories, and then I returned north. What actually happens is so tenuous: who we meet and when.

The despair was overwhelming.

The arguments were the same and valid: you have lived long enough; death is not optional: it is only a matter of now or a few years from now: no acceptable future is possible; with a new variation: you have destroyed too much. I could not refute any of them. The contrast between the joy I had known: the voyages, the women, the writing; and the joyless present and future. Watching television and playing computer games are not being in love or sailing around Cape Horn. I should have died with RESURGAM, I thought. It was the right time to die, the right way. If not the right place. Better farther from land, better somewhere in the Southern Ocean. But still I would have disappeared at sea. The only thing I did wrong was survive once too often.

The counterpoint was only that the despair was so overwhelming, it was self-defeating. Motion was nearly impossible. Going to the bathroom, turning on the television, walking two blocks to the store to buy more Lean Cuisine meals every three or four days. Two more rejection slips of *Circles* arrived and did not help. They actually did not matter that much either. I had already given up that hope, the weeks of writing in the New Hampshire mountains already added to years of futile effort.

And my personal myth: you are capable of greatness; you are one of those aberrations thrown out of the gene pool to go beyond established limits; to struggle to the end. You still have money, about $23,000, and therefore time.

The part of me that wanted to live knew I had to get out of Key West.

I had not come south with any intention of buying a boat. The idea had presented itself at a used car dealership in Miami, when I thought that for the price of this piece of junk, I could buy a boat. It had been reinforced in Key West by the sight of sails off the beach and boats anchored where Jill and I had anchored RESURGAM, and an increasing desire to have my own space, my own home again.

I managed to pull myself together sufficiently to buy some magazines and newspapers. I found an ad for a job teaching sailing for the summer on Long Island Sound. I found an ad for a boat for sale in Connecticut that might be interesting: a 36 feet ultra-light weight splinter designed for the solo transatlantic race, a freak; but then it had to be for me to be able to afford it.

I called an auto transport company. There is no shortage of cars to be driven to New England from Florida in April. I gave away my bicycle. Carried three bags and a knapsack to the car—in Key West I had bought a swimming suit, even though I didn't leave the beach, two short sleeved shirts, a portable CD player and about twenty CD's. I was becoming wildly acquisitive. And drove north.

In early afternoon I stopped for a sandwich in Fort Lauderdale. Back on I-95 it took me two hours at seventy miles an hour before I saw the exit sign for Sebastian. I thought: it is not possible I was in the water all that distance.

As I drove north I felt myself approaching Jill. I felt her presence only a few miles away. I felt as though I could reach out and touch her. I wanted to go by her parents' house and take her with me. I thought how a single word from her could change my life so completely, as it had before.

I drove to South Carolina before I stopped.

Each morning, not long after dawn, the gunfire resumed. A single shot cracked out over the usually still and, in that deceptive light, lovely slate-colored water, followed by other shots, combining to form rapid fire volleys. Commands barked over loud-speakers. I am not an expert, but often they used automatic weapons. Occasionally I heard the deep cough of something of much larger caliber. And bombs. Smoke rising in thick columns into the air, ash falling from the sky, covering the deck. Some days the detonations were continuous for more than an hour.

This was not Somalia or the former Yugoslavia. So it must be the Bronx. In a life of uncertainty, nothing was stranger to me than becoming a New Yorker.

I did not buy the boat in Connecticut.

Prior to seeing it, my concerns were about its design and construction, but in fact the owner/designer/builder had done a good job. Although light, the boat was strongly reinforced and seemed sound. It would certainly be fast. But the interior was a disaster, and the boat was ugly. I had been warned that it had only five feet of headroom. There was even less. And, worse, the entire cabin, sole, overhead, sides, was covered with mismatched scraps of indoor-outdoor carpeting.

After the years in an open boat, I thought I could live on and sail anything. But CHIDIOCK TICHBORNE had been a pretty little boat. This was a pretty boat only to a moth.

I asked the owner why after going to the trouble of designing and building a boat expressly for the solo transatlantic race, he did not ever sail the course. The man said his wife wouldn't let him.

Despite its defects, I tried to convince myself to buy the boat. I spent two nights aboard at the marina. The interior was dark and depressing. There were few places I could even sit up straight. It was like living inside a damp carpet.

I had planned to sail thirty miles west to City Island, where the sailing school was located, and live at anchor while teaching for the summer.

I telephoned the school and told the director that I had no place to stay and could not afford New York rents. The director, desperate for someone with a Coast Guard license, said I could sleep on one of the school's teaching boats. I drove over and moved onto a 28-foot sloop.

City Island is a real island, about a mile long and three streets wide, reached only by a bridge, near the boundary between the Bronx and Westchester County. It dangles like a pancreas in the western extremity of Long Island Sound, a body of water known in summer for its flat mirror-like surface. This is probably just as well, for off the Bronx you do not want to see what is beneath that surface.

Gunfire is commonplace around New York City. Although most of the gunfire is sincere, that around City Island is merely practice. For New York, City Island is a fairly safe place. The sailing school was only broken into once that summer. The NYPD's outdoor shooting range is at adjacent Rodman's Neck, where all the city's weapon-carrying employees have to qualify yearly. Explosives, such as those seized after the World Trade Center bombing, are also stored and disposed of at Rodman's Neck. Naturally the residents of City Island are thrilled about this.

Once City Island was one of the great yachting centers of the world. As a boy growing up in the Midwest, I knew the names of the boat yards there. Olin Stevens, who designed RESURGAM, opened his first office on City Island. America's Cup contenders were built there as were yachts for the Astors and Vanderbilts. But those days ended decades ago. Nevens is closed. Olin Stevens moved to Manhattan long before he retired. And in the worst travesty, Minneford's name now graces a showroom for candy-flake painted powerboats.

The boat yard where the sailing school was located was itself once a builder of fine boats. In my first days at City Island I called the yard a floating slum; but after a few weeks of rowing ashore, I described it more accurately as a semi-floating slum of half-submerged docks, broken pilings, and wrecks. One old power vessel that covered and uncovered with each tide could have been a stand-in for the AFRICAN QUEEN.

There were still boats there and some distinguished old houses, one of which was used for the filming of Long Day's Journey Into Night. City Island is dwarfed by its past, as for that matter is all of New York City, and perhaps America.

On most days, but not all, the skyline of Manhattan is visible ten miles or so to the west of City Island. By car those towers are between thirty minutes and several hours distant, the variables being rush hour and the bottomless potholes on the misnamed expressways.

One of the advantages of New York is that you don't need a car. But City Island is beyond the farthest extremities of the subway. Via public transportation Manhattan is more than an hour away. You take a bus from City Island for the first two or three miles to reach the end of the Number 6 line at Pelham Bay Station. Then you ride on the surface for several miles before descending below ground.

On the subway I was again in a foreign city. Not until stops around Ninetieth Street in Manhattan is English spoken. And every moment, above ground and below, one is constantly confronted by ugliness. There is beauty in New York, but it is isolated and artificial and carefully nurtured. Beauty in New York is a momentary oasis in a vast desert of ugliness.

You can find anything in New York. The city never sleeps. Or so they say. I know people who wouldn't live anywhere else. Yet it requires a very peculiar mentality to do so, a mentality that demands limitations, to be constantly surrounded by millions of other people, never to have open horizons. To dream in New York, one must turn inward and shut doors to lock out the city. In New York even on the water, I missed the open sea.

Riding back to City island from Manhattan one evening about 9:00 p.m., I had an unexpected experience. About eight stops from the end of the line, I realized that I was alone in the subway car. After nose to nose jamming in Manhattan and the lower Bronx, everyone else had disembarked. Leaning forward I looked up and down into the adjacent cars. As far as I could see I was alone on the train.

The train pulled into stations, doors opened automatically onto empty platforms, then automatically closed, and the train sped onward into the night, slowed at the next station and the eerie process was repeated. I had fallen into the Twilight Zone.

Years alone at sea had not prepared me for the dark heart of the Bronx.

I enjoyed teaching sailing for a while. I had done so in San Diego that summer almost twenty years earlier between my attempts at

Cape Horn. I generally like people who like boats. It was interesting to rethink something I know well and see it through the eyes of students. Most of my waking hours were filled. My life was stabilized until October.

Few of the students knew who I was, but the other instructors did and could not believe I was there.

Being on the water again was quietly satisfying, even that water. I liked rowing out to the mooring in the evenings after work and ashore in the mornings. I liked having the moat between myself and the land. Occasionally I could even see the stars and the moon.

The Laser 28 I was living on was not bad, but my few possessions had to be stowed out of the way on the quarter berth when I went ashore each morning, so the boat could be used for teaching. There wasn't much space. The quarter berth was the only one long enough for me to sleep on. It was free housing, but it wasn't very satisfactory. Tahiti and Cape Horn to the Bronx, I thought. How far I have fallen.

Mondays and Tuesdays were my days off.

The first two weeks, I rode the subway into Manhattan to see movies and to shop. I saw *The Crying Game*, and I bought a 2" Sony TV and a Sony multi-band radio receiver. With cheap quartz watches and the Global Positioning System satellite technology, navigators don't really need time signals any longer, but I like to listen to the BBC in mid-ocean. From the very beginning, even when purchasing the notebook computer that first month in New Hampshire, before I had any intention of returning to the sea, I did not buy anything that would not fit or operate on a boat.

Starting with my third set of days off, I rented cars and drove to Connecticut and Long Island to look at boats. An ad in *Soundings* led me three hundred miles north to Vermont. Upstate New York, Vermont, New Hampshire, Maine, continued to be a revelation of beauty to me. If I were not a sailor, I thought I could live there. I drove north through unexpectedly pristine forests, skirted Lake George, reminiscent of Switzerland, and crossed into Vermont's farmland.

The yacht broker had told me to turn west at Shelburne, Vermont's one traffic light. I did and found myself on a country road. For a couple of miles there was no evidence that water was anywhere near, and then I caught a glimpse of Lake Champlain, just before the road curved to end at the Shelburne Shipyard. Not boat yard, as I had been corrected at the Texaco station at the traffic light. Shipyard.

They do not build ships there any longer, but it is a big modern facility, with hundreds of boats, in and out of the water of a rock and pinetree lined cove. HAWKE was in a cradle out of the water. My first thoughts were: she is big. And obviously she is green.

Boats always look bigger out of the water. HAWKE has a deep fin keel with a 6'6" draft, several inches more than any other boat I have owned, and a wide 12' beam. Of course she is built of fiberglass. I admire wood boats, but people who own wood boats want to work on them, not sail them. HAWKE's hull was laid up in December 1975, when I was first rounding Cape Horn. She had been sailed only a fraction of the miles of RESURGAM; but as I walked around her, staring up at her hull painted 'jade mist green' with two gold stripes at the waterline and a gold cove stripe near the deck ending in a rather nice depiction of a hawk, tail near the stern, head near the bow, I saw evidence that she had been raced with more than reckless abandon. That and her stripped out racing interior were the reasons I could even consider buying her. Prices on used boats were soft in 1993. HAWKE was listed at $30,000, but she had been on the market for more than a year, and the broker said he thought she would sell in the low twenties.

I had been looking at smaller boats which would cost almost as much. I could live on them by myself, but they were too small for a couple. HAWKE was big enough for two people, if I found a woman again.

I did not like the interior, but it could be improved. She had an old Volvo diesel. There was a worrisome repair to the mast. She was far from perfect, and I was very aware as I inspected HAWKE of what I had destroyed in RESURGAM.

I knew that I could not really afford HAWKE. Boats always cost more than their asking price. I could see ten to fifteen thousand more dollars I would have to spend to make her into a blue water home, capable of sailing anywhere. Money I did not have. Still she was pretty and basically sound. She could be a start, something I could rebuild upon.

As I drove back down to the city, I thought of HAWKE sitting there covered by snow the preceding winter, while I was at Bill and Hemmie Gilmore's house a hundred miles due east. I had gone a long way south only to come back.

The next week I drove to Vermont to look at HAWKE again. The mast still worried me, but I had taken bigger risks. I made an offer of $22,000 and bought the flawed green sloop for $22,500.

Alone aboard HAWKE at City Island after powering through the Champlain Canal and down the Hudson River, I did not feel quite as I had expected. Partially it was that in getting to know her, I realized how much I had done over the years to make RESURGAM mine and how much I would have to do to HAWKE. But partially it was that we were still surrounded by land.

True there was a way to reach an open horizon, but it lay either west through Hell Gate and down the East River or a hundred miles east around Long Island. Bridges, houses, the skyline of Manhattan. One of the functions of cities is to conceal the natural world from those who do not want to confront it, and we were surrounded by one of the most concealing cities on the planet.

When the school closed in October, I headed HAWKE west to Hell Gate and Sandy Hook. I breathed a little easier as a fair wind filled in behind us, our bow wave began to sing, and the New Jersey shore vanished. Still all the way south, we were making a coastal passage. Land was never more than one hundred miles away, and HAWKE was not at sea more than a week at a time.

In Beaufort, I touched RESURGAM's track in 1989, and again in St. Augustine. But it was in Fort Lauderdale that I truly closed that particular circle and confronted the past.

I had planned to sail over the approximate position where RESURGAM sank ten to twelve miles offshore; but the wind was light as I approached from the north and the gesture seemed empty.

I went directly into Port Everglades and north on the Intracoastal Waterway to the tiny mooring area near the Las Olas Bridge. There I tied to a vacant mooring, which happened to be next to the one RESURGAM occupied on her penultimate night afloat.

I pumped up the inflatable and rowed to the landing, then

walked east over the Las Olas Bridge and looked down at HAWKE, just as I had fifteen months earlier looked down at RESURGAM.

They are similar boats, with semi-flush decks. HAWKE a bit bigger, in theory a bit faster, and with a green hull; RESURGAM burgundy, elegant, perfect, veteran of all oceans and Cape Horn. I pictured her for a moment, only a few miles away, beneath a thousand feet of water, fish swimming through her open hatches. I cared for her and trusted her as I did not yet care for or trust HAWKE. But she was gone, irretrievably gone, and, in time, I thought, I might come to care for this stranger, which I had not then renamed. After circumnavigating in EGREGIOUS, CHIDIOCK TICHBORNE, and RESURGAM, I thought I was tired of explanations and that someone else's HAWKE would remain HAWKE. But by the time I painted her topsides teal a few years later, I had put so much of myself into modifying the sloop, I decided she was sufficiently mine to change her name to THE HAWKE OF TUONELA, a variation on the title of a piece of music by Jean Sibelius.

A few days later I sailed to Key West. Entering the harbor, I passed the beach where I had sat staring out to sea earlier in the year.

There is a considerable difference between having sailed around the world once and not having sailed around the world at all. But there isn't much difference between sailing around the world four times rather than three. Still I need goals and I could again consider myself halfway through my fourth circumnavigation. It will be something if I can put one more over on time and chance.

Little more than a year had passed since I lost everything except my life. In New York I reread some of Jan de Hartog's books. In one of them he wrote, "Old men should be explorers." At 51 I was only middle-aged. When I came from the water after twenty-six hours in August 1992, I did not expect to have another boat so soon. Or live in the Bronx. Or be back in Key West. But I had sufficiently recovered to put everything at risk once again. And, though harbor bound, I was closer to finding sea room again and, I hoped, love.

ACKNOWLEDGMENTS

I wish to thank Patience Wales for her generous introduction and Lothar Simon for providing me with this valedictory opportunity as I prepare to sail from my literal to my true native land.

Over the years various parts of this book have appeared in many publications. They include: SAIL, Cruising World, Yachting, Fort Lauderdale Sun-Sentinel, San Diego Union Tribune (U.S.); Yachting World, Yachting Monthly (England); Voiles et Voiliers, Neptune (France); Modern Boating (Australia); South African Yachting (South Africa).

Other books of interest from Sheridan House

ADVICE TO THE SEALORN
by Herb Payson

"No other writer can capture the cruising life—the dreams and reality, the heartaches, the humor, and even the philosophy—the way Herb does.... From selecting the right boat to dealing with storms, guns, money, and other uncertainties, Payson will calm your fears as he revs up your cruising dream. " *SAIL*

FLIRTING WITH MERMAIDS
By John Kretschmer

"The glamorous life of a professional sailor? Here's the straight story, with humor, salty adventures, and a steep learning curve."
Gregory O. Jones, editor, *Sailing*

"Not only has John Kretschmer lived a life wildly festooned with adventure, romance and outrageous characters.... but the sailor can write. It's a hell of a read." Fred Grimm, columnist, *Miami Herald*

HANDBOOK OF OFFSHORE CRUISING
by Jim Howard

"For those who dream, as all serious sailors do, about stepping beyond the coast in their voyaging, a book which covers every detail—from idea to casting-off and beyond is a great place to start....This is not a beginning sailor's book or a travel book. It is a guide to the thousands of choices and compromises that must be considered and made in sailing beyond the coast." *Journal of the American Sailing Association*

MAYDAY!
by Joachim Schult

"Here is satisfying adventure reading combined with practical analysis of what put yachts in distress and how it might have been avoided. The book is full of stories and lessons not only about storms, personal terror and aberrant personalities, but about the groundings and simple carelessness that can befall any ordinary boater. Read it for entertainment or for knowledge, you are sure to be pleased either way. " *Dockside*

A SEA VAGABOND'S WORLD
by Bernard Moitessier

"...a priceless work as straightforward and unpretentious as the man who composed it.... No essential topic is left untreated, and the result is a unique window into the way Moitessier the master solved problems that voyagers in the tropics confront all the time.... The read is personable and easygoing, the format eclectic enough to make every page jump out at you with something new and instructive. " *Blue Water Sailing*

America's Favorite Sailing Books
www.sheridanhouse.com